CISTERCIAN FATHERS SERIES: NUMBER FIFTY-THREE

BERNARD OF CLAIRVAUX

SERMONS FOR THE SUMMER SEASON
Liturgical Sermons from Rogationtide and Pentecost

CISTERCIAN FATHERS SERIES: NUMBER FIFTY-THREE

Bernard of Clairvaux

SERMONS for the SUMMER SEASON

Liturgical Sermons from Rogationtide and Pentecost

Translated, with an Introduction, by
Beverly Mayne Kienzle
additional translations by
James Jarzembowski

Cistercian Publications
Kalamazoo, Michigan
1991

This translation is based on the critical edition prepared by Jean Leclercq, H. M. Rochais, and C. H. Talbot, *Sancti Bernardi Opera,* volume 5: pages 121–216 (Rome: Editiones Cistercienses, 1968).

The work of Cistercian Publications is made possible in part by support from Western Michigan University to The Institute of Cistercian Studies

The editors express their gratitude to John Leinenweber for his editorial help in preparing the manuscript for publication.

Library of Congress Cataloguing-in-Publication Data:

Bernard, of Clairvaux, Saint, 1090 or 91–1153.
    [Sermones per annum. English. Selections]
    Sermons for the summer season: liturgical sermons from Rogationtide and Pentecost / Bernard of Clairvaux; translated by Beverly Kienzle.
        p. cm. — (Cistercian Fathers series; no. 53)
    Translated selections from: Sermones per annum.
    Includes indexes.
    ISBN 0-87907-153-2. — ISBN 0-87907-453-1 (pbk.)
    1. Pentecost season—Sermons. 2. Rogation days—Sermons. 3. Catholic Church—Sermons. 4. Sermons, Latin—Translations into English. 5. Sermons, English—Translations from Latin.
    I. Kienzle, Beverly Mayne. II. Title. III. Series.
    BX890.B5375 1990
    252'.67—dc20
                                                             90-44119
                                                                  CIP

Printed in the United States of America
Typography by Ideas In Graphics

In loving memory of my mother,
Virginia Cleveland Mayne, and in
gratitude for her many gifts, her
sparkle, and her example of tireless
commitment to the tasks she undertook

table of contents

preface

Emendemus in melius

TO FIX THIS TRANSLATION onto the printed page is to stop short a process that has occupied some portion of my work or thoughts for the last several years. I feel, as perhaps does any translator of an important writer, that the process of emendation could go on indefinitely, that to end it is to deliver a text whose revisions are necessarily incomplete. *Emendemus in melius*, the Lenten antiphon that Jean Leclercq has used to describe the spirit of Bernard's revisions, expresses my thoughts on being a translator of Bernard. It also points out the enormous debt that I, as anyone who studies Bernard, owe to the works of Jean Leclercq.

We know, from Jean Leclercq's research, that Bernard was intensely preoccupied with revising his own works for the precision of vocabulary, the quality of his Latin grammar, and the euphony or musicality of the words. The translator faces the task of conveying in modern English the key words that express Bernard's thoughts, the complex interrelatedness of his ideas, and finally the sheer energy of his language and his delight at manipulating words. How does one render the cogent, controlled force of a lengthy Latin sentence into a modern language that values conciseness? Or how does one capture Bernard's careful yet playful love of alliteration and other wordplay? He says in Sermon Two for the Sixth Sunday after Pentecost that while he was breaking the bread of his thoughts into *fragmenta*, many *frustra* passed through his fingers. He gathers both—*frustra* and *fragmenta*, mouthfuls and morsels—into his sermon. His translator must settle for letting some of those crumbs fall, for it is not possible to find an English equivalent for every instance of Bernard's wordplay. At times figures of speech are lost in order to make content clear.

I wish to thank the several people who have assisted me in preparing this volume. Father James Jarzembowski's clear and forceful translation of the first seven sermons was an invaluable guide in my revisions. I am exceedingly grateful to John Leinenweber, OSB who carefully and graciously edited the text, making corrections and suggestions, checking and adding references, and even reviewing the introduction. I am also grateful to E. Rozanne Elder who guided the book from editing my very first samples to answering countless questions and putting on the finishing touches. I also wish to thank John R. Sommerfeldt who read the Introduction and offered insights and references from his own work in preparation. My students at Harvard Divinity School read some of the translations in class and they too, especially Susan Shroff and Anne Thayer, deserve thanks for the thoughtful questions that helped to analyze the texts.

Friends and family have provided much encouragement—the late Father Eugene A. Green who often rekindled my enthusiasm and helped me to plan the project's early stages; my parents, Virginia and Lewis Mayne, who proudly supported my work, even during some vacation visits, and who first gave me a love of learning; my aunt, Ann Cleveland, who is equally thrilled over all my projects; my daughter, Kathleen, who patiently let me slip into the quiet of my study and even helped me proofread; and my husband, Edward, who supports all my work with generous enthusiasm, listening to ideas, proofreading, and shouldering more than his share of household chores.

B.M.K.

introduction

BERNARD OF CLAIRVAUX was the dominant figure of the twelfth century and one of the most influential people of the Middle Ages.[1] Monk, abbot, renowned preacher, adviser to the powerful, participant in controversy, he is remembered primarily as a writer and teacher. Born in 1090 to a family of the lower nobility, he entered the monastery at Cîteaux at the age of twenty-three, and within three years of his arrival was named abbot of Clairvaux, Cîteaux's third foundation. During Bernard's forty years as a Cistercian, the Order experienced phenomenal growth and influence. His first published writings appeared around 1125, and he continued to write extensively. He also became involved in church affairs, defending the claims of Innocent II to the see of Rome against Anacletus, preaching the Second Crusade, and engaging in theological debate with Abelard and other leading thinkers. During his last years he devoted himself to rewriting his vast works, among them the liturgical sermons included in this volume.

THE LITURGICAL SERMONS AND
THEIR MANUSCRIPT TRADITION

Among Bernard's extant works are some one hundred and twenty liturgical sermons. These sermons were first published by Jean Mabillon, *Sancti Bernardi abbatis Clarae-Vallensis Opera Omnia* (Paris: Gaume, 1839), which were then reproduced by J-P. Migne in the *Patrologia Latina* (vol. 153). Jean Leclercq, Henri Rochais, and C. H. Talbot have prepared a new edition of all Bernard's works, *Sancti Bernardi Opera* (Rome: Editiones Cistercienses, 8 vols. in 9, 1957-1977). The sermons presented in this volume are translations of the Leclercq and Rochais text, volume 5, and comprise the nineteen sermons from Rogation through the season of Pentecost.

---

1. For a recent biographical sketch of Bernard with sources for his biography, see Michael Casey, *Athirst for God: Spiritual Desire in Bernard of Clairvaux's Sermons on the Song of Songs,* CS 77 (Kalamazoo: Cistercian Publications, 1988), pp. 3-17.

The manuscript tradition for Bernard's liturgical sermons has been described at length by H. Rochais and J. Leclercq.[2] It will be useful to present here a summary of their conclusions as they pertain to the sermons in this translation. Rochais and Leclercq distinguished four great series for the liturgical sermons: B (*brevis*), M (*media*), L (*longior*), and Pf (*perfecta*).[3] All the liturgical sermons and therefore all the sermons in this volume are included in the Pf series manuscripts. One sermon in Mabillon's edition but not in Pf (VI p P2) was eliminated by Leclercq and Rochais, and two in Pf, formerly in Mabillon's *De diversis*, were added: Ascension 5 (Div 43) and On the Heart's Loftiness and Baseness (Div 36). Most of the sermons here appear in more than one series and three (Asc 4, P P 3, Pent 1) appear in three of the four. The manuscript series for the sermons is summarized in the table on page 7 which also includes the length of each sermon.

The Pf series is considered one that Bernard edited, choosing among existing texts and revising them, introducing new ones, and ordering all of the texts according to the liturgical year. Since all the liturgical sermons belong to the Pf series, all were edited by Bernard himself late in his life. The dates established for the series L and Pf, after 1148 and after 1150 respectively, indicate that Bernard undertook a careful revision of his greatest works, including the liturgical sermons, during the last years of his life.[4] Like the *Sermons on the Song of Songs*, then, the liturgical sermons represent carefully crafted works of literature.[5]

2. 'La tradition des sermons liturgiques de S. Bernard,' *Scriptorium* 15, 2 (1961) 240-73; SBOp 5: xi-xiv. For the *Sermones de diversis*, see also H. Rochais, 'Enquête sur les sermons divers et les sentences de Saint Bernard,' ASOC 18 (1962) 1-182.
3. B, L, and Pf also correspond to editions of the sermons on 'Qui habitat.'
4. 'Tradition des sermons liturgiques,' p. 276.
5. See also Jean Leclercq, 'Were the Sermons on the Song of Songs Delivered in Chapter?' Introduction to *Sermons on the Song of Songs II*, trans. Kilian Walsh, CF 7 (Kalamazoo: Cistercian Publicatons, 1983) vii-xxx. In his articles on Bernard's style, J. Leclercq uses numerous examples from these liturgical sermons. See, for example, 'Sur le caractère littéraire des sermons de S. Bernard,' *Studi Medievali* 7 (1966) 718, 720, 726-27; and 'Essais sur l'esthétique de S. Bernard,' *Studi Medievali* 9 (1968) 710, 712-14, 716, 719-20, 722, 724. Dorette Sabersky also uses examples from these liturgical sermons in her *Studien zur Paronomasie bei Bernhard von Clairvaux*, Freiburger Zeitschrift fur Philosopie und Theologie (Freiburg, 1979) pp. 119, 164, 180, 188, 204-05. Etienne Gilson has remarked that Bernard renounced everything but the art of writing well; see *La théologie mystique de Saint Bernard* (Paris, 1947) p. 81.

WRITTEN OR ORAL FORM

Still one can legitimately ask to what extent Bernard's oral preaching is reflected in these sermons. Even in the *Sermons on the Song of Songs* there is some relationship between the written text and Bernard's preaching.[6] Certainly we would expect liturgical sermons, rooted in Cistercian daily life, to reveal something of an oral preaching tradition. But any conclusions about sermons examined more than eight hundred years after the event of their writing or possible preaching must necessarily be tentative.

BERNARD'S METHOD OF COMPOSITION:
Qui scribit, certis rationibus collocat universa

Jean Leclercq has given us a way of analyzing Bernard's and other twelfth-century sermons, and has studied at length the oral and written characteristics of Bernard's style in the *Sermons on the Song of Songs*. He considers Bernard's *Sentences* or sermons in brief the clearest examples of the warm and intimate talks Bernard delivered during chapter. These *Sentences* were not composed in writing but were delivered orally and then written down in note form by listeners. The notes from the chapter talks were then reworked in a more polished form and inserted in longer literary works. Consequently, the style of certain sermons evidences some passages much closer to the spoken word than others, and some that present theological arguments too complex to have been spoken.[7]

Method of Analysis

For the *Sermons on the Song of Songs*, Jean Leclercq examines extratextual evidence—the statements of Bernard's contemporaries—and intratextual evidence—sermon length, references to Bernard's public in the second person, first person singular references and whether they occur in the sermon openings and closings, and allusions to monastic community life.[8]

To summarize the intratextual evidence, a sermon that is too long to have been delivered during the Cistercian day, addresses

6. Leclercq, 'Were the Sermons...', pp. xxiii-xxiv.
7. See Leclercq, 'Were the sermons...?' pp. xiv-xvi, and 'The Making of a Masterpiece,' Introduction to *On the Song of Songs* IV, trans. Irene Edmonds, CF 40 (Kalamazoo: Cistercian Publications, 1980), p. ix. See also 'S. Bernard et ses secrétaires,' in *Recueil d'études sur S. Bernard*, I (Rome, 1962) pp. 3-25.
8 'Were the Sermons...?' pp. viii-xxiv.

the recipient in the second person singular, contains personal references in the opening or closing (both of which were tightly ruled by literary convention), and makes few allusions to daily life in the monastic community, is probably a literary work and not the transcription of a sermon delivered orally. Conversely, a sermon close to its oral form would be short, would address the community in the second person plural, would contain significant personal references (probably in the body of the sermon), and would contain direct allusions to monastic life.

My own observations, on Bernard's and other medieval sermons, strongly support Jean Leclercq's view of Bernard's method of sermon writing and his insistence that the sermons, the liturgical ones as well as those on the *Song of Songs*, are developed literary works. In its early stages, research on Hélinand of Froidmont's *Chronicon* and sermons reveals a writer borrowing material from his *Chronicon* to use in a sermon and also inserting an earlier written sermon into the *Chronicon*.[9] While some of Hélinand's sermons were delivered on identifiable occasions, the text we possess is too long and too complicated to have been delivered.[10] One manuscript of Hélinand's sermons also contains what appear to be sermons in brief,[11] like the sentences of Bernard. This evidence, like Jean Leclercq's for Bernard, indicates that monastic writers of the twelfth and early-thirteenth centuries kept track of their notes and their works, borrowed from and revised what they had already written, and displayed varying degrees of carefulness that reflected their concern for the aesthetic quality of their writing. In Sermon Four for the Ascension, a sermon that appears in three of the four manuscript series, Bernard himself provides us with a description of the writer who tries to order words in a way that reveals divine mysteries: 'Just as a writer arranges everything for specific reasons, so the things that

9. See for example PL 212:721 where Hélinand states, 'sermonem in conventu fratrum edidisse me memini in hunc modum.' This passage is found in Book Eight of Hélinand's *Chronicon* and is part of the *Flores*, excerpted from the *Chronicon* by Vincent of Beauvais. I am grateful to Edmé R. Smits, University of Groningen, for that information.
10. See for example Ascension Fifteen, delivered in Toulouse. The text occupies just over fifteen columns in the Migne edition.
11. Paris, Bib. Maz. 1041, fols. 72-96.

are from God are appointed; and especially those performed by his majesty present in the flesh.'[12]

Sermon Length
   The first factor to analyze for the sermons in this volume is their length. The sermons can be divided into four groups according to the number of lines in the Leclercq-Rochais edition: A, 27-73 lines; B, 88-115 lines; C, 139-150 lines; D, 214-256 lines. The chart below indicates how many lines each occupies (without title and rubrics) and summarizes the manuscript information presented earlier.

SERMON	NUMBER OF LINES (GROUP)	MANUSCRIPT SERIES
Rogation	35 (A)	M, Pf
Ascension One	62 (A)	M, Pf
Ascension Two	115 (B)	M, Pf
Ascension Three	150 (C)	M, Pf
Ascension Four	254 (D)	B, M, Pf
Ascension Five	27 (A)	L, Pf
Ascension Six	256 (D)	M, Pf
Pentecost One	104 (B)	B, M, Pf
Pentecost Two	143 (C)	M, Pf
Pentecost Three	144 (C)	M, Pf
John the Baptist	214 (D)	M, Pf
Peter and Paul, Vigil	61 (A)	Pf
Peter and Paul, One	88 (B)	Pf
Peter and Paul, Two	139 (C)	B, Pf
Peter and Paul, Three	103 (B)	B, M, Pf
Fourth after Pentecost	98 (B)	L, Pf
Sixth after Pentecost, One	73 (A)	Pf
Sixth after Pentecost, Two	111 (B)	Pf
Heart's Loftiness and Baseness	69 (A)	Pf

   Group A contains six sermons; group B six; group C, four; and group D, three. Some sermons stand out as being too long for delivery: those in groups C and D are significantly longer than the median length of 104 lines, those in D being more than twice the median. All of these lengthy sermons belong to at least two

12. Asc 4, 2; SBOp 5:139: '...qui scribit, certis rationibus collocat universa.'

manuscript series. The sermons in group A are short enough to be preached; those in B are probably too long but are short enough to be close to an earlier and shorter oral form. Three of the six sermons in group A belong only to the Pf series, and two of the six in group B belong only to the Pf series.

For the *Sermons on the Song of Songs*, Jean Leclercq concluded that most could not have been preached as we have them because they take up at least four to five columns in the Migne edition and thus would require a full hour or more to deliver or read aloud.[13] Checking the length of these liturgical sermons in the Migne edition corroborates my conclusions. Group A sermons occupy two columns or less; those in group B take up about three columns; those in group C fill four to five columns; and group D sermons extend over six to seven columns.[14]

Forms of Address

Examining the forms of address used in the sermons in this volume allows for extending Jean Leclercq's conclusions. While forms of address may lead us to discover passages that have an oral source, forms associated with oral delivery may also have been added to give the impression of an oral setting. Emero Stiegman has pointed out that in the *Sermons on the Song of Songs*, Bernard mimics an oral presentation,[15] and that is certainly possible in these sermons as well. Hence forms of address are not in themselves reliable indicators of original oral form but are perhaps included to approximate the delivered sermon as closely as possible. And, on close examination, the forms of address considered signs of oral setting (first person singular and, especially, second person plural) reveal complex patterns of usage.

In searching for personal references, one looks for the use of the first person singular. The first person singular combined with the second person plural gives an impression of an oral situation when, for example, Bernard is speaking directly to his monks about their vocation. In Asc 2,5, he says: 'Does anyone know whether all of you whom I see here have your names inscribed

---

13. See 'Were the Sermons Delivered?,' p. xv.
14. PL 183: 297-344, 397-416, 637-38, 665-66.
15. 'The Literary Genre of Bernard of Clairvaux's *Sermones Super Cantica Canticorum*,' in *Simplicity and Ordinariness*, ed. John R. Sommerfeldt, CS 61 (Kalamazoo: Cistercian Publications, 1980), pp. 73-74.

in heaven...?'[16] But whether in openings, closings, or the body of the sermon, first-person references are often formulaic and parenthetical. Sermons contain first-person formulae that reflect patterns of thought in speech or composition (*inquam, ni fallor, dico, dicam,* etc.) and tell us nothing about the oral or written source of the text.[17] The first person singular is also used to introduce the interpretation of a text: *arbitror, credo,* and similar words likewise indicate nothing decisive about oral or written form.[18] Any first person singular reference must be weighed according to its content and to norms for literary composition.

The use of the first person plural is no more telling than that of the first person singular. One might expect the first person plural, especially when joined with *fratres,* or *dilectissimi,* to represent an oral exhortation to the monastic community, and perhaps it sometimes does. But first-person plural references are often part of the sermon's closing exhortation and thus closely governed by literary conventions.[19] Within the body of a sermon, there is sometimes a transitional exhortation; that is, when completing one idea and before moving to the next, Bernard exhorts his public to implement what he has just explained.[20] And the words *fratres* or *carissimi,* which might seem to indicate direct address and thus an oral form, are not reliable indicators. In these sermons, they do appear with forms of address in the first person plural and second person plural, but once *fratres* follows closely after two verbs in the second-person singular![21]

16. SBOp 5:129.
17. For example: Asc 4, 1; SBOp 5:138: 'Dico ergo vobis;' Asc 4, 6; SBOp 5: 142: 'ut arbitror;' Asc 6, 8; SBOp 5:154: 'ni fallor;' Pent 1, 5; SBOp 5:163: 'Dixeram;' PP 3, 2; SBOp 5:199: 'aliud habeo quod apponam...;' PP 3, 6; SBOp 5:201: 'meministis, credo... meministis, inquam....' These last second-person plural forms follow four second-person singular forms in the same section.
18. The first person used for interpretation is found in Rog, 1; SBOp 5:121: 'Amicum... non alium intelligo quam meipsum.' Here also Bernard's identification with the gospel text is strong; he states 'Ego [sum] mendicus' twice. Again for the interpretative first-person, see IV p P, 2; SBOp 5:203: 'Credo... non incongrue'; and 204: 'Arbitror... non incongrue.'
19. See, for example: Rog, Asc 1, Asc 2, Asc 3, Asc 5, JB 12, PP 2, VI p P 1.
20. An example of a transitional exhortation is found in JB, 7; SBOp 5:181-82.
21. In Asc 1, 1, Bernard shifts from 'Audis...' (line 2), 'Noli...' (line 4) to 'Sed quid est, fratres...' (line 7). Examples of *fratres* with second and first plural are frequent, for example: Asc 1, 2: 'Sed quid ad haec dicemus, fratres'; SBOp 5:124; Asc 2, 3; SBOp 5:127: 'Quid tamen putatis, fratres.'

Shifts between Second Person Singular and Plural

In some sermons Bernard shifts from second-person plural to second- person singular, or vice versa.[22] If the plural form were used to address the community and the singular to address a reader, does a shift from plural to singular in the text represent a move from one source text to another as Bernard compiled the final version of his sermons? That is, did he put aside a source very close to its spoken form and take up another composed originally for reading? Such a conclusion is tempting and perhaps justifiable in long sermons. Ascension Four, for example, has many second person singular references, but the first half of its section nine contains several second-person plural references.[23] Bernard has just finished speaking to the children of humankind (*filii hominum*) and then calls upon his brothers directly (*Obsecro vos, fratres mei...*), beseeching them to put aside worldly concerns and meditate on heaven. Certainly that section of the sermon reflects an oral form of address that is deliberate if not originally spoken. A careful study of the three manuscripts in which Ascension Four appears could yield a firmer conclusion about the source of this passage, but that is beyond the scope of this introduction.

Some shifts from second person plural to singular seem to indicate a deliberate change in Bernard's focus. He moves from the community as a whole to each person as an individual. That shift would reflect a situation of oral delivery and could reveal a text close to its oral form—or the author's desire to approximate an oral form. Perhaps a reading of English 'you all' for the plural and 'you each' for the singular would be helpful to understand the workings of such a passage. While this pattern remains to be tested in other liturgical sermons, some examples follow that illustrate its workings in a sermon from this collection.

'On the Heart's Loftiness and Baseness' is a short sermon, present only in the Pf series and formerly in Mabillon's *De diversis* collection. It focuses clearly on monastic community life—the Rule's instruction to endure each other's weaknesses with patience, and the grumblings that result when the Rule is moderated for some. Of the sermon's four sections, the first and the

---

22. See for example PP 3, VI p P 2.
23. SBOp 5:145-46: pronouns and adjectives: 'vos,' 'vestra', 'vos,' 'vestra,' 'vestra,' 'vestris,' 'vos,' 'vestra,' 'vos;' and verbs: 'Exonerate,' 'sciatis,' 'Levate,' 'videatis,' 'formate,' 'circuite,' and 'habeatis,' before shifting back to the second person singular.

second use the second person plural (except for a formulaic *Quantum putas...* in the second); the third and the fourth use the second person singular extensively. In the third section, Bernard tells a story he admits he has told before about a lay monk.[24] After the story, he expresses his hope that each of the monks meditate on the higher things which constitute the fullness of humility. Here he uses eight verbs and four pronouns in the second person singular.[25] He then uses the first person plural to express wishes and obligations for the community.[26] In the fourth section he also uses the second person singular and ends with a statement in the first person plural.[27] The message conveyed in the second person singular has to do with personal meditation—how to remain in a humble state by reflecting on the strength of another rather than on one's own good qualities. Thus the shift from the plural to the singular form seems better explained here by a shift in focus than by a switch from one source text to another. This is yet another reminder that content must be considered along with linguistic clues.

BERNARD'S *PERSONA* AS PREACHER

Bernard's preoccupation with the aesthetic quality of his language is closely tied to his concern for content. Jean Leclercq has pointed this out[28] and one of the sermons from this collection illustrates it clearly. In Sermon Two for the Feast of Peter and Paul,[29] Bernard expresses the worry that his message of salvation might not be heeded. At the same time he justifies his need

24. The story is also told in the *Exordium magnum*. See SBOp 5: 215.
25. SBOp 5:215: 'attendas,' 'tibi,' 'fueris,' 'te,' 'poteris', 'potes,' 'te,' 'videris,' 'versaris,' 'Esto,' 'scias,' 'tibi.'
26. SBOp 5:215-16: 'essemus,' 'debuimus,' 'debuimus,' 'desideramus,' 'possimus.'
27. SBOp 5:216. Second person singular forms are: 'praeponis,' 'negligis,' 'arbitraris,' 'incipis,' 'tibi,' 'videris,' 'incidis,' 'incipis.' The first person plural forms are contained in a future more vivid conditional sentence: 'mortificaverimus,' 'vivemus,' 'vixerimus,' 'moriemur.'
28. See especially 'The Making of a Masterpiece,' pp. xvi-xxiii.
29. I discussed Bernard's second sermon for Peter and Paul in a paper presented May 10, 1990 at the Bernard Nonacentenary sponsored by the Institute of Cistercian Studies, Kalamazoo, MI: 'The *persona* of the Preacher in Bernard's Liturgical Sermons.' The final version of the paper, '*Verbum Dei et Verbum Bernardi*: The Function of Language in Bernard's Second Sermon for Peter and Paul,' will be published with selected papers from the Nonacentenary edited by John R. Sommerfeldt.

to speak and to reproach his community. And his choice of words shows great care in composition. The motive, the message, and the method are fused to give us a picture of Bernard's *persona* as preacher, a role that combined his concerns as abbot, teacher, and writer.[30]

Here Bernard uses first-person singular references that go beyond such formulaic language as parenthetical remarks, introduction of an interpretation, or comments pertaining to the length of a sermon. He interjects personal reflection, somewhat like a narrator who does not shed his or her personality but enters into the story, making references to self, and sometimes explaining why something is being told in a particular way. Just as the narrator generally is more concerned with story than with self, so the preacher is more concerned with the message of salvation than with self. And while the narrator inserts the first person into the text to be sure that the story is reaching the audience, the preacher intervenes in the text out of concern that the message be conveyed. Yet this text reveals careful composition: what is deeply felt is not, for Bernard, expressed spontaneously, that is, in the spontaneous outbursts that our own day associates with sincerity.[31]

Here Bernard's intervention in the sermon text is tied to his awareness of the limitations of language, and to his deep sense of his responsibility as abbot for the spiritual dimension of the lives entrusted to him.[32] While he clearly loved words, especially God's words which he says are the fruits of life, he was acutely aware that those words which are repeated with frequency may not be heeded. Thus he justifies to his listeners his need to repeat certain things, and to reproach them at times and tell them

---

30. Emero Stiegman speaks about the *persona* of abbot, 'The Literary Genre,' pp. 80-82.
31. Jean Leclercq has observed that Bernard's plays on words often serve as a psychic release, freeing a spiritual tension. 'Essai sur l'esthétique,' p. 706. And Christine Mohrmann has stated: 'Son style reflète exactment ce qui se passe en lui.... A mesure que le niveau s'élève, le style devient plus orné et plus mouvementé.' But she also points out that late in life, Bernard's style became more simple and sober. 'Observations sur la langue et le style de saint Bernard,' Introduction, SBOp 2: xxv.
32. Bernard's ways of advising his monks in the sermons recall his styles of spiritual direction. See William O. Paulsell, 'Bernard of Clairvaux as a Spiritual Director,' Cst 23, 3 (1988) 223-31.

what they doubtless did not want to hear. And he strives to vary the language and enrich the imagery in order to express his timeless message with words that command notice.

Sermon Two for the Feast of Peter and Paul begins with what Bernard says is a digression (sections 1-3). He expresses concern that the words of salvation, when heard over and over again, may become worthless and like leaves float out of the listener's mind. The rhythm of his speech conveys the motion of the leaf blown about in the wind, and the use of alliteration evokes the sounds of the breezes.[33] His language in this passage is intensely figurative, calling further attention to his message.[34] He asserts that God's words are the fruits of life, and he refers to the parable of the barren fig tree (Lk13: 6-9) that, if still barren after applications of dung, should be axed. For dung, although filthy, brings fruitfulness. He then brings the image to life and personalizes it, taking on the role of the vineyard keeper obliged to dig about since he has been appointed to a position of responsibility. He states that he is not unaware that a chiding word is like manure; unless needed, it makes the one speaking it less comely. But some are enriched by the manure of reproach and attempt to change their lives, while others are assaulted, perceiving the manure as stones, and persisting in sinful ways. A just reproach should be taken with a kind spirit and with gratitude to the chider. Whatever pertains to salvation should be heard kindly, received devoutly, and preserved carefully. Bernard feels that he has digressed wisely if the lesson has been learned. He then turns to the feast itself for the remainder of the sermon.

The theme of the first half of Sermon Two for Peter and Paul and its imagery appear elsewhere in Bernard's works. The subject of Sermon Forty-Two on the Song of Songs, for example, is also fraternal correction. Bernard speaks of his obligation to reproach and states that he fulfills the role of prophet and apostle although he considers himself unworthy of either.[35] In Sermon Sixty-Three on the Song, he develops the vineyard and tree

33. SBOp 5:191-92: 'verum,' 'verba,' 'vilescere,' 'verba,' 'Vilis,' 'volatilis,' 'verbum,' 'verberat,' 'verbum,' 'vento.' Note also the rhythm of 'nullius morae, nullius ponderis, nullius pretii, nullius soliditatis,' etc.
34. Christine Mohrmann traces this figurative style back to Gorgias, but its influence is due to Augustine who gives it its perfection and theoretical justification, 'La langue,' p. xi.
35. *Song of Songs II*, pp. 210-19.

imagery with reference to a just person, and then compares young novices to trees in blossom and not yet bearing fruit.[36]

Further examples of Bernard's personal reflections on his responsibility are also found in four other sermons in this collection. In two of those Bernard justifies his duty to rebuke members of his community from the position of his authority as successor in the role of Christ and the apostles. In Sermon One for the Ascension (section one), Bernard points out that Christ rebuked the disciples' disbelief and hardness of heart just at the moment when he was about to ascend, leaving them saddened, and when reproaching them might have seemed least appropriate. Bernard then advises his audience that in the future they should not be angry if he, Christ's representative in the monastery, reproaches them. He is only doing for them what Christ did for his disciples. Sermon One for the Sixth Sunday after Pentecost is based on Mk 8:1-9. Bernard interprets each of the three days passed in waiting with Christ. He relates to himself and his listeners the order given the apostles to make the people sit down (Jn 6: 10). This sitting down is necessary so that love may be ordered in them. Bernard admits that it perplexes him, the representative of the apostles, to be the one who must admonish them to sit down. But the purpose of his admonition is clear and necessary, if they are to persevere in their journey and not go down into Egypt, that is, if they are to remain faithful to their monastic vocation (section two).

Bernard's responsibility to receive complaints and grant dispensations enters into 'On the Heart's Loftiness and Baseness,' discussed above. When dispensations are granted to the weak, others may grumble, stirring up suspicions and scandals. Bernard explains that his desire to forewarn his monks and avoid such problems is the reason for addressing the topic in the sermon. He has no particular complaint, but past experience with individual monks has shown him that some do not easily forgive the weaknesses of others (section two).

36. *Song of Songs III*, trans. Kilian Walsh and Irene M. Edmonds, CF 31 (Kalamazoo: Cistercian Publications, 1979) p. 166. Paul Meyvaert points out this passage and other garden imagery used by Bernard in 'The Medieval Monastic Garden,' *Medieval Gardens*, Dumbarton Oaks Colloquium on the History of Landscape Architecture, IX, ed. Elisabeth B. McDougall (Washington, D.C.: Dumbarton Oaks, 1986) p. 49.

Finally, in the Sermon for the Feast of John the Baptist, the obligation to reproach when necessary is widened to include the community. Bernard justifies his responsibility, and also advises his listeners that in certain matters they share this responsibility with him. He calls on the fearless example of John the Baptist, reminding his audience that each one is his brother's keeper. He urges them not to keep silent and calm when discipline is being weakened in the Order, because when someone can rebuke, to be silent is to give consent, and doers and consenters alike will be punished (section nine). This specific reference to the Cistercian Order may indicate that this passage was once delivered to Bernard's monks, although the sermon as a whole is very long and could not have been delivered as it now exists. Certainly the audience for this passage was Cistercian and not a wider public.

OVERVIEW OF THE SERMONS

The sermons in this collection are rich sources for studies on Bernard's style and thought. To underscore their richness, the remainder of this introduction provides a brief summary of each, calling attention to major themes and to some remarkable images. Throughout these sermons we feel the pull of Bernard's experiential spirituality, his call to introspection and meditation. Whatever the liturgical season, scripture is intimately related to the inner life. Timeless images take on the context of monastic culture and the wider framework of introspective meditation: bread, water, wine, light and darkness, bride and bridegroom, the royal road, footsteps and the journey, the desert, the heavenly city. The audience for Bernard's message is clearly monastic, and the sermons manifest what has been called a spiritual elitism.[37] Yet in some cases, especially when the subject is the life of Christ, the Christian in the world can set aside the specifically monastic context and focus on Bernard's call to introspection and meditation. While meditating on Christ's humanity was for Bernard only a first spiritual step, imitation of holy example, and especially of Christ, is a prominent feature of these sermons. John Sommerfeldt points out that the *Sermons on the Song of Songs* also contain many reflections on the life of Christ and that although Bernard

---

37. See Bernard McGinn, 'Resurrection and Ascension in the Christology of the Early Cistercians,' *Cîteaux* 30 (1979) 15.

assigned the highest place to meditation on God, most of the reflections he shared with others concerned meditation on the life of Christ.[38]

The Rogation Sermon, the first in this collection, is based on the story of the importunate friend in Luke 11; its theme is Luke 11:5-6: 'Who among you shall have a friend and go to him in the middle of the night to say: "Friend, lend me three loaves, because a friend of mine has come to me from his journey, and I have nothing at all to put before him." '[39] The sermon is structured around the three loaves. Bernard supposes that three people are arriving: the friend, his wife, and a servant. He interprets the friend at home as himself, a beggar, with no bread in the house; the man coming from his journey is his reason, the wife is his will, and the servant is his flesh. The three loaves are truth, charity, and fortitude, which must be asked for, and, when received (Lk 11: 10), nourish the reason, will, and flesh so that one may understand, love, and do God's will.[40]

Bernard's fondness for the feast of the Ascension is reflected in the number and length of the Ascension sermons; there are six, and two among them are the longest in this collection. Bernard recalls the events of Christ's life and passion that have their fulfillment in the Ascension. He exhorts his audience to *meditatio* and *imitatio Christi*, to ponder the life of Christ and

38. 'Meditation as the Means to Humility in the Thought of Bernard of Clairvaux,' delivered at the 24th International Congress on Medieval Studies, Western Michigan University, May 6, 1989, and part of a longer work in preparation, *The Spiritual Teachings of Bernard of Clairvaux*, to be published by Cistercian Publications in 1990. I am very grateful to John Sommerfeldt for providing me with a copy of his work. Marsha Dutton also remarks that meditation on Jesus points the way to the Godhead; see 'Eat, Drink and Be Merry: The Eucharistic Spirituality of the Cistercian Fathers,' in *Erudition at God's Service*, ed. John R. Sommerfeldt, CS 98 (Kalamazoo: Cistercian Publications, 1987) p. 14.
39. Jean Leclercq points out that reminiscences of the prodigal son's return are mixed with those of the friend. 'Essais sur l'esthétique,' p. 719.
40. For Rogation Bernard draws on the tradition of the Major Litanies. Cf. Bede, *In litania majore*, Hom. VIII; PL 94:168-74, where the three loaves represent the cardinal virtues. Augustine makes that association in S. 105, 5; PL 38:620. The Rogation Liturgy in the Molesme Breviary drew on sources for the Major Litanies; see Chrysogonus Waddell, *The Summer Season Molesme Breviary* I (Kalamazoo: Cistercian Publications, 1985) p. 39.

examine the deepest parts of their inner selves in order to live and suffer with Christ, and in the end to ascend to him.[41]

The first Ascension sermon begins with Mk16:14: 'While they reclined at table, Jesus appeared to the eleven disciples. And he rebuked their disbelief and hardness of heart, because they did not believe those who saw that he had risen.' Bernard then proceeds through Mk 15-18, reflecting on each verse separately. This scriptural theme generates several brief considerations. What is the significance of Jesus' appearance to the disciples while they were at table (verse 14)? Why would he be rebuking them when he was about to leave them (verse 14)? Who were those who saw that he had risen (verse 15)? Finally, is too great an assurance offered by the promise of salvation in return for baptism and belief (verse 16)? His concern about moral responsibility is centered on people of the world, certainly in the sense that they are less enlightened than monks about matters of faith. Verses 17-18, setting forth the signs of belief, receive more lengthy reflection; Bernard relates each of the signs to the inner lives of his audience. Demons are cast out through compunction of heart[42] when sins are rooted out. Believers in Christ speak in new tongues and confess their sins. Serpents are picked up when poisonous propositions are extinguished so that there is no relapse into sin. Not being harmed by drinking poison means that believers will refuse to swallow the poison, that is, refuse their consent to sin. Finally, curing diseases means that believers will be cured by acting on their own diseased dispositions (*aegras affectiones*) with good deeds.

Fulfillment is the theme of Sermon Two for the Ascension: Christ in his Ascension reaches the end of his journey as the Son of God; and the liturgical feast is the consummation of all the others. Eph 4:10 is the pericope: 'The one who descended is the very one who ascended above all the heavens to bring all things

---

41. J. Leclercq emphasizes the balanced attention in Bernard's theology to Christ's humanity and divinity; see 'Le mystère de l'ascension dans les sermons de Saint Bernard,' Coll.15, 2 (1953) 81-88, translated into English in Cst 25,1 (1990) 9-16; and Bernard McGinn stresses that for Bernard the risen and ascended Christ is the goal of the religious life; 'Christology,' p. 7. J. Leclercq points out that Bernard takes up themes from the Ascension sermons in SC 76, 1-5 and Div 60 and 61. McGinn points out Div 33 as well.
42. On compunction in Bernard, see Michael Casey, *Athirst*, pp. 123-29.

to fulfillment.'[43] Christ had already proven that he was Lord of all on the earth, in the sea, and in the lower regions; and with his Ascension, he proved that he was Lord of the air and the heavens. Also in this sermon, Bernard imagines the glorious procession which accompanied Christ as he took his seat at the right hand of God.[44] His dwelling in heaven completed the seamless garment and brought the integrity of our faith to wholeness. Bernard asks his brothers to empathize with the fear and grief of the apostles, and expresses his pain at not being a witness himself. But the promise of the second coming consoles him. Yet no one knows whether salvation or damnation awaits, and so Bernard urges his audience to persevere in their monastic discipline and practice the humility which alone leads to exaltation and eternal life. Foolish are they who seek out the high places of this world, the ecclesiastical offices that even the angels would fear to shoulder. Far better it is to be drawn or led by God's commandments, and even better still to be caught up by a spirit of ardor.[45]

Sermon Three, like Sermon Six, reflects on the understanding and the inclination (*De intellectu et affectu*).[46] Bernard envisions

---

43. According to Bernard McGinn, Asc 2 and 4 attempt general statements on the doctrine of redemption. Eph 4:10 and Jn 3:13 form a descent-ascent motif, the first of three in Bernard's teaching on the role of Christ according to the spirit. 'Christology,' pp. 10-11.
44. J. Leclercq points out that Bernard introduced an Ascension procession at Clairvaux. The information is contained in Hélinand's *Chronicon* for the year 1151 (PL 212:1057D). See Leclercq, 'Etudes sur S. Bernard,' ASOC 9 (1953) 154.
45. On the Third Heaven, see Michael Casey, *Athirst*, pp. 289-91.
46. I have chosen to translate *affectus* here as 'inclination(s)' when it denotes a feeling that inclines the will (*voluntas*) toward a certain action; that is, *affectus* in those cases is a subtle disposition that influences the will itself and is influenced by the passions. The distinction between inclination and will is seen clearly in Asc 3, 8, where *voluntas* and *affectus* are close in meaning, but distinct: 'for then your inclination (*affectus*) will be purified, and your will (*voluntas*) renewed.' In Asc 3, 1 *affectiones* is used synonymously with *affectus*: 'I think that [our] inclinations (*affectiones*) are called 'soul' here, for in a perishable body they are influenced by the different passions, which can never be mitigated, much less quieted.' But *affectus* is the word used throughout the sermon for this part of oneself that must be purified. In Asc 3, 4, *affectus* denotes a faculty synonymous with the will itself: '[Christ] sent the Holy Spirit, who purified their inclination (*affectum*), that is their will (*voluntatem*).' In still other cases and in other sermons, *affectus* is the feeling that inclines one toward God. Michael Casey summarizes his and other translators' renderings of *affectus* and *affectio* in *Athirst*, pp. 94-110.

Christ passing into heaven and putting on a robe of glory. Thus Christ, the Wisdom of God, returns to the land of wisdom where everyone's understanding is acute and everyone's inclination is intent on hearing God's word. In contrast, we dwell in a land of great wickedness and little wisdom, where 'the perishable body presses down the soul and the earthly dwelling burdens the mind that ponders many things' (Ws 9:15).[47] Bernard develops Sermon Three from this verse, interpreting 'soul' as the inclination and 'mind' as the understanding. The two parts of ourselves— understanding and inclination— must be cleansed: the understanding enlightened by Christ so that it may know the truth, and the inclination purified by the Holy Spirit so that it may will the good. Christ enlightened the understanding of the apostles when he opened their minds to understand the scriptures, and he sent the Holy Spirit to purify their inclinations, or their wills, so that they no longer wanted to detain the Lord, but preferred that he ascend. Turning to his community, Bernard advises them that their understanding has been enlightened, but that their inclinations have not equally been purified. Some are barely dragged to monastic exercises, and others are scarcely compelled by fear of hell. He urges them to renounce consolations of the flesh, to let sorrow fill their hearts, that it may be turned into joy, and their inclination be purified and their will created anew. All should weep and pray that the Bridegroom send the Spirit of truth, and that the Spirit fill the house where they are seated. Focusing on Christ[48] and the apostles for his examples, Bernard also draws on Elijah and Elisha and Enoch and Elijah as types.[49]

In Ascension Sermon Six (section 5), an image from contemporary life poignantly clarifies the soul's grievous torment when

---

47. An interesting study could be written on Bernard's use of this verse. See, for example in this collection: SBOp 5:122, 128, 131, 151, 155, 239, 401 ; and SBOp 4:206, 348, 351, 430, and 484.
48. Bernard McGinn notes that Asc 3 and Asc 6 also include the Augustinian theme of *conformatio* to Christ: Christ established a form to which we might be imprinted. 'Christology,' p. 14.
49. On Enoch and Elias, see Richard Kenneth Emmerson, *Antichrist in the Middle Ages: A Study of Medieval Apocalypticism, Art and Literature* (Seattle, 1981), pp. 95-101; and on Enoch and the Ascension, see Eugene A. Green, 'Enoch, Lent and the Ascension of Christ,' in *De Ore Domini: Preacher and Word in the Middle Ages*, ed. Thomas L. Amos, Eugene A. Green, and Beverly Mayne Kienzle (Kalamazoo: Medieval Institute Publications, 1989), pp. 13-25.

the understanding and the inclination are pulling it in opposite directions. This painful wrenching is likened to the physical torture experienced in the stocks, when a person's legs are pulled apart by a block of wood. Bernard remarks that everyone sees this public torture, and anyone's failing to heed it belies a destructive and dangerous lack of attention.

In Sermon Four, Bernard reflects on the various ascents of Christ that precede the Ascension: the mountain of the Transfiguration (sections 7-9);[50] the mount where he spoke the beatitudes (section 10); the mountain where he went up alone to pray (section 11). He adds two other ascents: Christ's mounting the beast of burden (section 12), and his ascent onto the cross (section 13). Bernard explains how each of these stages provides instruction on the self-preparation necessary for spiritual progress and aspiration to the final ascent. The mountain of the Transfiguration shows how one ought to ponder celestial glory; the mount of the beatitudes teaches how to meditate on the Lord's law; and the mount where Christ prayed alone gives instruction on praying for the right disposition for journeying and reaching the end. To mount the beast of burden, Bernard says, one ought to trample down bestial impulses. To follow Christ onto the cross, one must view as a cross what the world desires, and fully embrace what the world views as a cross. But there are also false ascents. The natural desire to strive after height leads many to climb a wicked mountain seeking after power, like Satan, or after knowledge, like Adam. Satan and Lucifer fell by trying to ascend that wicked mountain, but Christ descended in order to ascend.[51]

Ascension Five is brief, the shortest sermon in this collection. Bernard discusses the three virtues—courage, forbearance, and concord—possessed by apostles waiting for the Spirit. Those three virtues are signs of faith, hope, and love and must be imitated to obtain the Spirit in the measure that runs over.

There are three sermons for Pentecost and four for the Sundays following. With their structure insofar as possible based on groupings of three, the three Pentecost sermons reflect in form

50. On the significance of this Eastern feast to monks and its introduction to Cluny by Peter the Venerable, see Jean Leclercq, *The Love of Learning and the Desire for God: A Study of Monastic Culture,* trans. Catharine Misrahi (New York: Fordham University Press, 1982) p. 57.

51. Bernard McGinn points out this paradox of Christ's descent and its statement again in Div 60, 'Christology,' p. 12.

as well as content the mystery of the Trinity. Sermon One concerns how the Spirit assists us so that we may turn from evil and do what is good. For turning us from evil, the Spirit brings about compunction, petition, and forgiveness. For doing good the Spirit influences the three faculties of the soul, admonishing the memory, instructing the reason, and moving the will.[52] In this way the Spirit possesses the entire soul, and will fill the entire house at the end, in the judgment and resurrection when the days of Pentecost are fulfilled and our spiritual bodies rise.

In Sermon Two, Bernard explains the actions of the Trinity in us. He has Christ speak in the first person, saying that he gives us every stage of his life from his conception to his ascension and sending of the Holy Spirit. He was conceived of the Holy Spirit to cleanse our conception, he lived to instruct our life, he died to destroy our death, he rose to herald our resurrection, he ascended to prepare our ascension, and he sent the Spirit to assist our weakness. Thus we will see clearly the three aspects of our journey: the way to walk, the care with which to walk, and the destination. In Christ's life we recognize our way, and we must walk in his footsteps. In his death we receive his righteousness. His return to heaven directs us there, and in his absence the Spirit gives us the pledge of salvation, the force of life, and the light of knowledge. Thus we are taught all things concerning salvation.

Sermon Three contains the image of the Spirit as wine poured from heaven, extending the idea of exchange between heaven and earth,[53] that is, Christ came to earth, taking on our nature, and then the Spirit came when Christ returned to heaven. After expounding on the Spirit's proceeding from both Father and Son, Bernard asks his listeners to ponder three things about the world:

---

52. Bernard's division of the soul into memory, reason and will is noteworthy since he does not ordinarily uses this Augustinian division, but usually divides the soul into the three faculties of intellect, will and feelings (*affectus*). I am grateful to John Sommerfeldt for this insight from his forthcoming book, *The Spiritual Teachings of Bernard of Clairvaux.*

53. Bernard uses the word *commercium* here, as in the antiphon, 'O admirabile commercium,' for Vespers on January 1, Feast of the Holy Mother of God. On the antiphon and the exchange principle, see Frans Josef van Beeck, *God Encountered: A Contemporary Catholic Systematic Theology,* 1 (San Francisco: Harper and Row, 1989) pp. 63, 82-87.

what it is, how it exists, and for what purpose it was established.[54] Sense-bound persons reflect only on the first thing; the vain (philosophers according to Bernard[55]) consider the second; and spiritual persons meditate on the third. Bernard rejoices that his listeners are of the third school, where they may learn goodness, discipline, and knowledge, and may be able to understand the threefold Spirit: holy, 'right', and 'ruling'.

Following the Pentecost sermons are those for the Birth of John the Baptist, the Vigil of Peter and Paul, and three for the Feast of Peter and Paul. The John the Baptist sermon is built around Jn 5:35 : 'He was a burning and shining lamp.' Bernard examines the significance and relationship of the two words. It is nothing only to shine, and not enough only to burn; to burn and shine is complete: John burned from his own fervor and also shone for others. His splendor came from his fervor, not his fervor from his splendor. He burned with the rigor of his way of life, with the fervor of his devotion to Christ and with the constancy of his reproaches to sinful neighbors. He shone in his example, in pointing out Christ, and in his word; he showed himself so that we might imitate him.

This sermon contains a marvelous image (section 11) likening the memory stained by sin to parchment that has been so completely soaked in dregs that it is impossible to scrape it clean. For sin that remains in the memory reproaches its owner forever. This would be its state without the coming of John who announced the Lamb of God who takes away the world's sin. In an age and place where tanning was commonplace, one can image the strength of this image that relates the mind to the work of the monastery preparing skins, doubtless for the many codexes that Bernard's own writings would fill.

A secondary theme of the sermon for John the Baptist (section 6) receives more attention on the Vigil of Peter and Paul. Bernard decries excessive feasting. Inappropriate to celebrate the Baptist's birthday, self-indulgent celebrating contradicts the true purpose of vigils. For keeping vigil means remaining awake to sin, not

---

54. Bernard also speaks about meditation on the created things of the world in V Nat 3, 8; SBOp 4:217. I am grateful to John Sommerfeldt for this reference.

55. On Bernard's occasional expression of distaste for philosophers, see Michael Casey, *Athirst,* p. 36.

falling asleep in disgrace. Three things ought to be considered on the feasts of saints: their aid, their example, and our own shame. Here Bernard emphasizes the greatness of Peter and Paul; while we rejoice at their advocacy, we are ashamed at the difficulty of imitating them.

In Sermon One for Peter and Paul, Bernard considers Peter and Paul as teachers, but also points out their sins. They learned the paths of life from the Master of all, and they teach us how to live. For those in Bernard's community, living well is to live in an orderly, friendly, and humble manner. Sermon Two, as discussed above, begins with Bernard's reflections on his obligation to give constructive criticism; he is the vineyard-keeper applying manure to the fig trees. He then explains that the day's feast, unlike the Baptist's honoring his birth, commemorates the death of the two apostles. Bernard appeals to his brothers to live as Peter and Paul did, but even more to die as they died, having prepared themselves with wisdom, understanding, and prudence. Sermon Three focuses on Si 44:10: 'These are men of mercy.' Peter and Paul were men of mercy because they received mercy, were filled with mercy, and were mercifully given to us by God. Bernard returns to each of the apostle's great sins, advising anyone who has sinned to rise up and trust that forgiveness will not be denied so long as sin is confessed from the heart. He then takes up again the benefits of Peter and Paul's teaching, their lives, and their deaths.

The story of David and Goliath forms the basis of the sermon for the Fourth Sunday after Pentecost when the historical books of the Old Testament were being read at the Office. Bernard retells the story from the point of view of the listener's emotive reactions to the events. Here he uses verbs in the first person plural, giving at least the impression of an oral setting. Then searching for the kernel inside the wheat, he delights in looking for further meaning in the figure of Goliath.[56] Goliath not surprisingly represents the vice of pride. How can anyone defeat pride as David killed Goliath? Not with means such as secular wisdom or the surface of divine scripture, but with David's five stones which should be understood as the five kinds of words: warning,

56. Bernard also discusses searching for the allegorical sense of scripture in SC 73, 1-2; SBOp 2:234; SC 51, 2; SBOp 2:84; and SC 1, 9; SBOp 1:7. I am grateful to John Sommerfeldt for these references.

promise, love, imitation, and prayer. David's sling, long-suffering, is also necessary for this comflict. Finally one detail of the story remains: how to cut off Goliath's head with his own sword. Bernard explains this briefly, saying that he speaks to the experienced (a clear reference to a monastic audience). To cut off Goliath's head with his sword, one destroys vainglory with vainglory and regards oneself as humbly and as abjectly as one does Goliath.[57]

There are two sermons for the Sixth Sunday after Pentecost. The first is based on Mk 8:1-9, the feeding of the crowd with seven loaves. Bernard explains the significance of the crowd's three-day wait with Christ, and interprets each of the seven loaves. The three days are fear, holiness, and reason—the days of the journey in the desert that must be undertaken to offer a pleasing sacrifice to God. The seven loaves, which Bernard explains hurriedly, are: 1. the Word of God; 2. obedience; 3. holy meditation; 4. the tears of those who pray; 5. the labor of repentance; 6. pleasant social concord; and 7. the Eucharist.

Sermon Two continues the theme of another sermon on the loaves, but clearly not the preceding one, because the seven loaves are interpreted differently: 1. God's saving grace; 2. God's awaiting; 3. God's mercy; 4. God's forgiveness; 5. abstinence; 6. the grace of deserving the good things of eternal life; 7. the hope of obtaining. For each loaf, Bernard continues to play with the imagery of eating[58] and says that he offers various mouthfuls or morsels of bread (*frustra, fragmenta*), advising his listeners that these mouthfuls and morsels slipped through his fingers while he was breaking the loaves.

The final sermon, 'On the Heart's Height and Depth,' discussed above, refers to a text that Bernard says was just read, about how some look up and others down. Bernard addresses in a spirit of forewarning, he says, problems that arise in the community when dispensations are given for the weakness of one, causing envy

---

57. Jean Leclercq points out Bernard's use of stylistic crescendo here, culminating in this last blow: 'Goliam utique Goliae gladio peremisti'; 'Essais,' p. 722.
58. See Jean Leclercq, *Love of Learning*, p. 73 on the theme of spiritual nutrition and the related vocabulary of 'ruminatio.' In SC 7, 5; SBOp 1:34, Bernard uses saporous imagery to describe the way a psalm delights the heart. I am grateful to John Sommerfeldt for this reference.

in another. The fullness of humility requires that the brothers always be mindful of higher things. Bernard counsels them to be more mindful of what qualities they lack than of those they seem to possess; such thinking will preserve them in humility, prevent them from falling into lukewarmness, and enkindle in them a desire for improvement.[59]

As food for meditation by the faithful and as material for scholarly research, these liturgical sermons enrich our reading and make a connection between our worship and the liturgy of the early Cistercians. Rooted in the daily worship of monastic life, the sermons elucidate Bernard's profound vision and his pressing sense of responsibility to impart to others what the Holy Spirit made known to him. The motive of the abbot, the message of the teacher, and the method of the writer become one in the voice of the preacher. He calls his audience and us to an experiential spirituality—to relate scripture to the inner life through introspection and meditation. The spiritual lives of Christians in the world as well as those in the religious life can be strengthened by listening to Bernard's call.

59. The subjects of meditation—oneself, what is below and around oneself and what is above oneself—are explained in Bernard's advice to Pope Eugenius, (Csi 2, 3, 6; SBOp 3:414). Elsewhere Bernard states that humility results from meditation on oneself (SC 42, 6; SBOp 2:37); and that self-knowledge is enhanced by reflection on God's universe (SC 36, 6; SBOp 2:7-8). I am grateful to John Sommerfeldt for these references.

ROGATION DAYS

THE THREE LOAVES OF BREAD

WHO AMONG YOU SHALL HAVE A FRIEND,[1] and so on? Why is it that he says one friend has come, and yet is not content to request one loaf of bread? Do you suppose he reckoned the friend so ravenous that one loaf would not be sufficient for that one person? For it does seem wholly unreasonable to place three loaves of bread before one person. So conjecture then that the man arrived with his wife and his servant; and thus a friend would want to place one loaf before each of them.

I understand a friend who comes to me as none other than myself. No one, surely, is dearer to me; no one closer. Therefore, a friend comes to me from his journey[2] when I abandon transitory things and return to my heart, just as it was written: 'Return, transgressors to [your] hearts.'[3] Then at last one is truly a friend to oneself when one returns from the journey, because 'he who loves iniquity hates his soul.'[4] And so, from the day of my conversion, a friend has come to me from his journey. He came from a faraway land where he was accustomed to feed swine and to hunger insatiably for their husks. He came suffering from hunger, wasted from lack of food, and weakened from fasting. And he came needing to find a friend; but, ah me, he chooses an impoverished host and enters an empty dwelling place! What shall I do for this wretched and woebegone friend, for clearly 'I have nothing at all to put before him'?[5] I acknowledge that he is a friend, but I am a beggar. Why, my friend, have you come to me[6] in such urgent necessity? I am a beggar,[7] and there is no bread in my house.[8] Hasten, he says, run quickly, awaken that great friend of yours;[9] no one has greater love than he,[10] nor more ample provisions. Seek, ask, knock, because 'everyone who seeks finds, the one who asks receives, and to the one knocking, it shall be opened.'[11] Call out and say: Friend, lend me three loaves![12]

---

1. Lk 11:5   2. Lk 11: 6   3. Is 46:8
4. Ps 10:6 (11:5) The first number refers to the Vulgate psalter, used by Bernard; the second to versions translated from the Hebrew.
5. Lk 11:6   6. Gn 26:27   7. Ps 39:18 (40:17)   8. Is 3:7
9. Pr 6:3   10. Jn 15:13   11. Lk 11:10; Mt 7:8   12. Lk 11:5

2. What are these loaves, my brothers? Would that we deserved to receive them; for perhaps they are the very loaves 'no one knows, except the one who receives [them].'[13] Yet I believe that we ought to ask for the three loaves of truth, charity, and fortitude. I am in need of these three, I admit, when my friend is coming to me from his journey, and, as I said, coming with wife and servant. My reason is, of course, wanting—this is the man—because of my ignorance of the truth; my will, too, languishes because of the starvation of my affections; my flesh is weakened because of my want of fortitude. The reason understands none too clearly what is to be done, and the will loves none too ardently what is understood; and for these reasons 'the perishable body presses down the soul,'[14] and thus we do whatsoever we do not wish to do.[15] My heart has withered away, and my body, too, 'because I have forgotten to eat my bread.'[16] This defect would not have been evident, if [my] reason had continually been exercised in the search for truth, my will in the desire for charity, and my flesh in the practice of virtue.

Then 'lend me three loaves, friend,' that I may understand, that I may love, and that I may do your will.[17] 'By these things [people] live, and in them is the life of my spirit,'[18] as the Scripture says: 'because there is life in his will.'[19]

---

13. Rv 2:17   14. Ws 9:15   15. Ga 5:17   16. Ps 101:5 (102:4)
17. Heb 10:7, Ps 39:9 (40:8)   18. Is 38:16   19. Ps 29:6 (30:5)

the LORD's ascension

Sermon One
ON THE GOSPEL READING

WHILE THEY RECLINED AT TABLE, Jesus appeared to the eleven disciples.'[1] Truly the kindness and love of the Saviour appeared,[2] and he manifests great faithfulness, because if he does not refuse his presence to those who are reclining at table, he will be even more readily present to those who are inclined to prayer.[3] His kindness appeared, I say, [the kindness of him] who knew our making.[4] He has no scorn but rather compassion for our needs, if we make provision for the flesh not out of desire[5] but out of need. The Apostle has the same thing in mind when he says: 'Whether we eat or whatever else we do, we must perform all things for the glory of the Lord.'[6] Yet [Jesus'] appearance to [the apostles] as they reclined at table can also be compared to what [he says] on another occasion to the Jews who were finding fault with the disciples for not fasting: 'The bridegroom's friends cannot mourn as long as the bridegroom is with them.'[7]

[The text] continues: 'And he rebuked their disbelief and hardness of heart, because they did not believe those who saw that he had risen.'[8] You hear Christ reproaching the disciples, or rather even rebuking them, because he sounds quite harsh. [He did this] not just at any time, but at the moment when he was about to withdraw his bodily presence, [when] it might seem that he ought instead to have spared them his reproach. Do not be angry then in the future if at times Christ's representative should reproach you. He is conferring on you what [we] read that Christ conferred on his disciples when he was about to ascend from them into heaven.

But why is it, brothers, that [Mark] says: 'They did not believe those who saw that he had risen?' Who were they, whose blessed eyes[9] deserved to see the glorious miracle of the Lord's resurrection? [We] do not read or believe that any mortal saw him rising,

---

1. Mk 16:14, as in the former Mass of the Ascension.
2. Tt 3:4   3. RB 4: 56   4. Ps 102:14 (103:14)   5. Rm 13:14
6. 1 Co 10:31   7. Mt 9:15   8. Mk 16:14   9. Mt 13:16

and so we are left to take as angels those whose testimony to the resurrection[10] the apostles' irresolution doubted.

2. Now, in order that there be carried out what was written: 'Teach me goodness and discipline and knowledge;'[11] let the grace of his visitation, the correction of his rebuke, be followed by his instruction on preaching [the gospel], for he says: 'Whoever believes and is baptized will be saved.'[12] But what shall we say in response to these things, brothers? With this saying, too great an assurance seems to be offered to people of the world, and I fear lest they begin to render that assurance an opportunity for the flesh,[13] flattering themselves more than is appropriate on [their] baptism and belief apart from [good] deeds.

Nonetheless, let us consider what follows: 'These signs shall accompany those who believe.'[14] Perhaps the despondency these words occasion even in those in the religious life will seem just as great as the occasion for vain hope that the earlier words give to those in the world. Who then seems to possess the signs of belief written about in the passage at hand, without which no one can be saved? For 'whoever does not believe will be condemned,'[15] and: 'without faith it is impossible to please God.'[16] Who, I ask, casts out demons, speaks in tongues, or picks up serpents?[17] Does it not follow, then, that if in our times no one has these [signs], or few appear to have them, no one will be saved, or only those who boast of these gifts, which cannot so much claim a reward as provide evidence for such a claim? For that reason, as many are saying: 'Did we not cast out demons in your name and in your name did we not work many miracles?'[18] at the judgment they will be obliged to hear: 'I do not know you; go away from me, doers of iniquity!'[19] Where is what the Apostle says when he speaks about the righteous judge,[20] 'who repays each according to his deeds,'[21] if, perish the thought, signs are sought at the judgment rather than [other] claims to a reward?

3. Yet the claims themselves are also signs of a sort, doubtless more certain and salutary ones. I do not think it difficult to know how the signs in our present passage can be interpreted, that they may be unmistakeable signs of belief, and consequently [signs]

---

10. Ac 4:33   11. Ps 118:66 (119:66)   12. Mk 16:16   13. Ga 5:13
14. Mk 16:17   15. Mk 16:16   16. Heb 11:6   17. Mk 16:17-18
18. Mt 7:22   19. Lk 13:27   20. 2 Tm 4:8   21. Rm 2:6

of salvation as well. For the first deed of faith[22] acting through love[23] is compunction of heart; with it 'demons' are assuredly 'cast out' when sins are rooted out from the heart. Then those who believe in Christ speak in new tongues with the old [words] now gone from their mouths,[24] and they do not speak in the future with the ancient tongue of [their] first parents, who turned to words of wickedness to make excuses for [their] sins.[25] When their past sins have been effaced[26] by the heart's compunction and the mouth's confession,[27] then lest they suffer a relapse and their later sins be worse than their earlier ones,[28] they must 'pick up serpents,' that is, extinguish poisonous propositions. But what is to be done if for some reason a root sprouts and cannot be plucked out quickly enough, but excites the mind with a craving of the flesh?[29] Truly, 'if they drink anything deadly it will not harm them,'[30] because, following the Saviour's example, when they have tasted it, they will refuse to swallow;[31] that is, when they have sensed [the poison], they refuse their consent. Without consent, the sense of craving will not harm them, 'because there is no condemnation for those who are in Christ Jesus.'[32] What [will happen] though? Surely troublesome and dangerous is the struggle of a corrupt and weak disposition. But those who believe 'will lay their hands upon the diseased and they will be well.'[33] This means that they will act upon their diseased dispositions with good deeds,[34] and they will be cured by this remedy.

---

22. 2 Th 1:11 23. Ga 5:6
24. 1 S 2: 3, Wednesday Lauds, ferial canticle.
25. Ps 140:4 (141:4), Thursday Vespers.
26. Ac 3:19 27. Rm 10:10 28. 2 P 2:20; Mt 12:45
29. 1 Jn 2:16 30. Mk 16:18 31. Mt 27:34
32. Rm 8:1 33. Mk 16: 18 34. Mt 26:10

[the LORD'S ASCENSION]

Sermon Two
HOW [CHRIST] ASCENDED OVER ALL THE HEAVENS TO BRING ALL THINGS TO FULFILLMENT

OEARLY BELOVED, this solemn feast is glorious and, let me even say, gladsome, too; on this feast matchless glory is conferred on Christ and special joy on us. This is the consummation and the fulfillment of the other liturgical feasts, and this is the perfect ending to the Son of God's entire journey.

'The one who descended is the very one who ascended' today 'above all the heavens to bring all things to fulfillment.'[1] He had already proven that he was lord of all things[2] on the earth and in the sea and in the lower regions; he had but to prove with similar but surely stronger arguments that he was also lord of the air and the heavens. The earth[3] recognized [its] lord, because when he cried out in a loud voice: 'Lazarus, come forth,'[4] at the sound of his mighty voice[5] it restored the dead man. The sea recognized [him] when it provided a firm footing for his steps, and the apostles thought he was a ghost.[6] Even hell recognized [him] when he shattered its bronze gates and iron bars,[7] and bound therein that insatiable murderer [who is] called the devil and Satan.[8] Surely the one who raised the dead, cleansed lepers, gave sight to the blind and steadiness to the lame,[9] and chased away all infirmities with a breath, was lord of all, and with the same hand he had used to shape things, he was reshaping what had become misshapen. Likewise when he predicted that a coin would be found right in the mouth of a fish,[10] it was evident that he was lord of the sea and all things moving in it. He who put the powers of the air to public shame and nailed them to his cross had clearly received authority over the workshops of hell.[11] He it is 'who went about doing good and healing all who were oppressed by the devil,'[12] who stood firm on level ground[13] to teach the crowds and stood before the governor to endure blows to his

---

1. Eph 4:10　　　　　2. 2 M 14:35
3. Cf. Gregory the Great, *Hom. in Evang.* 10.2; PL 76: 1111AB.
4. Jn 11:43　　　　　5. Ps 67:34 (68:33)　　6. Mt 14:25-26
7. Ps 106:16 (107:16)　　8. Rv 20:2　　　9. Mt 11:5
10. Mt 17:27　　　　11. Col 2:14-15　　12. Ac 10:38
13. Lk 6:17

face.[14] All the while he was seen on earth and dwelt among humans[15] he stood firm amidst many labors,[16] working salvation throughout the earth.[17]

2. Lord Jesus, to complete your seamless garment,[18] to bring the integrity of our faith to its wholeness, you, lord of the air, have only to ascend in open air, above all the heavens[19] while your disciples look on.[20] This will prove that you are lord of the universe,[21] because you fulfilled everything in all things.[22] Accordingly, now it shall be your due that at your name every knee shall bend, in heaven, on earth, and in the lower regions, and every tongue shall confess[23] that you are in glory and at the Father's right hand. In his right hand are delights for evermore.[24] That is why the Apostle admonishes us to seek what is above, where Christ is, seated at the right hand of God.[25] There surely is our treasure, Jesus Christ, 'in whom all treasures of wisdom and knowledge are hidden,'[26] in whom all the fullness of divinity resides bodily.[27]

3. Brothers, how great in your estimation were the grief and fear that seized the apostles' hearts when they saw him carried from them and lifted into the air, unsupported by a ladder's rungs or by ropes, not even upheld by the ministering angels who accompanied [him], but marching in the greatness of his own strength?[28] What he had said to them was fulfilled: 'Where I am going, you cannot come.'[29] For anywhere on earth that he might have gone, they would have followed him inseparably; they would even have stepped into the sea with him to sink, as Peter once did.[30] But here they could not follow[31] because 'the perishable body presses down the soul, and this earthly dwelling burdens the mind that ponders many things.'[32] [Their] grief was unbounded because they saw him for whom they had left everything[33] being taken away from their senses and sight. With the bridegroom taken from them, the friends of the bridegroom could only mourn.[34] [Their] fear [too was unbounded] because

---

14. Jn 18:22
15. Ba 3:38
16. 2 Co 11:23
17. Ps 73:12 (74:12)
18. Jn 19:23
19. Eph 4:10
20. Ac 1:9
21. 2 M 14:35
22. Eph 1:23
23. Ph 2:10-11
24. Ps 15:11 (16:11)
25. Col 3:1
26. Col 2:3
27. Col 2:9
28. Is 63:1
29. Jn 7:34
30. Mt 14:29-30
31. Jn 13:36
32. Ws 9:15
33. Mt 19:27
34. Mt 9:15

they were left as orphans[35] in the midst of the Jews, not yet strengthened by the power from on high.[36] Then, blessing them, he was taken into heaven.[37] Perhaps his heart, matchless in mercy,[38] was stirred as he left his miserable ones, his poor band of disciples. But [he knew that] he was going to prepare a place for them,[39] and that withdrawing his bodily presence from them[40] was for their own good.

How happy, how fitting was that going forth, to which even the apostles were not yet worthy of being admitted! Led to the Father by a triumphal procession of holy souls and heavenly powers, he sat down at the right hand of God![41] Now has he truly brought all things to fulfillment:[42] he was born among humans, lived among humans,[43] suffered and died at human hands and for the sake of humanity rose, ascended, [and] is seated at the right hand of God. [In all this] I recognize that garment woven in one piece from top to bottom,[44] which this dwelling in higher realms has completed, for there the Lord Jesus Christ has attained fullness and has brought all things to fulfillment.

4. Still, what are these solemn feasts to me? Lord Jesus, who will console me? I did not see you hanging on the cross, bruised by beatings, pallid in death; I did not suffer with you when you were crucified, or honor [you] in death, that at least I might wash the place of [your] wounds[45] with my tears. Why did you leave me out of those farewells, on the day when, as the King of Glory,[46] robed in majesty,[47] you withdrew to the highest heavens? Admittedly my soul would have refused consolation[48] if angels had not come before me and with great rejoicing said:[49] 'Men of Galilee, why do you stand looking up into heaven?' This Jesus who has been taken away from you into heaven will come in the same way that you saw him go up into heaven.[50] 'He will return,' they say, 'in the same way.' Will he then come to seek us in that procession, as unique as [it is] universal, when, preceded by all the angels and followed by every person, he descends to judge the living and the dead?[51] Of course he will come, but in the way he ascended, and not as he earlier descended.[52] For he came first

35. Jn 14:18
36. Lk 24:49
37. Lk 24:50-51
38. Col 3:12
39. Jn 14:2
40. Jn 16:7
41. Mk 16:19
42. Eph 4:10
43. Ba 3:38
44. Jn 19:23
45. Jn 20:25
46. Ps 23:7-10 (24:7-10)
47. Is 63:1
48. Ps 76:3 (77:2)
49. Ps 46:2 (47:1); Is 48:20
50. Ac 1:11
51. 2 Tm 4:1
52. Eph 4:10

in humility to save souls;[53] but he will come in sublimity to raise dead bod[ies] and remake them bright and glorious like his,[54] so that the smaller and weaker the vessel, the more abundant the honor he may be seen to bestow.[55] For the one who was first concealed in the flesh's weakness[56] shall be seen then with great power and majesty.[57] And I too shall look upon him, but not now; I shall see him, but not near,[58] in such a way that this second glorification will shine manifestly brighter than the first on account of its surpassing glory.[59]

5. In the meantime he has been taken up to the right hand of the Father and now stands before God's countenance on our behalf. He sits at God's right hand,[60] holding mercy in his own right hand, judgment in his left: exceedingly great his mercy, and exceedingly great his judgment; immoveably he holds water in his right hand, and fire in his left. He has strengthened his mercy for those who fear him as 'heaven is high above earth,'[61] so that they can perceive the reaches of the Lord's mercies as greater than the distance between heaven and earth. For God's design for them[62] remains immutable and his mercy is 'upon those who fear him from eternity to eternity':[63] from eternity by reason of predestination, to eternity by reason of glorification. Likewise for the condemned, he is to be feared among the children of humanity.[64] [His] utterance remains fixed for eternity, on the one side and on the other, among those who are being saved and among those who are perishing.[65]

Does anyone know whether all of you whom I see here have your names inscribed in heaven[66] and recorded in the book of predestination? For in this humble way of life I seem to observe some signs of your calling and justification. How great a joy do you think would fill all my bones if I could succeed in knowing that? But no one knows 'whether he is deserving of love or hatred.'[67]

6. On that account, dearly beloved, persevere in the observance[68] you have undertaken, that through humility you may ascend to sublimity. This [is] the way, and apart from it there

53. Lk 9:56 in Vulgate and some Greeks texts.
54. Ph 3:21   55. 1 Co 12:23-24   56. Ga 4:13
57. Lk 21:27   58. Nb 24: 17   59. 2 Co 3:10
60. Ps 109:1 (110:1)   61. Ps 102:11 (103:11)   62. Rm 9:11
63. Ps 102:17 (103:17)   64. Ps 65:5 (66:5)   65. 2 Co 2:15
66. Lk 10:20   67. Qo 9:1   68. Heb 12:7

is no other. One who goes another way falls instead of ascending, because humility alone exalts and alone leads to life.[69] Christ, in his divine nature, had no way to grow or ascend, because there is nothing beyond God. Yet he found a way to grow by descending, coming to be incarnated, to suffer and to die, lest we should die forever. Because of this God exalted him;[70] for he rose, ascended, and took his seat at the right hand of God. 'Go and do the same.'[71] You cannot ascend unless you descend,[72] because it is fixed as by an everlasting law, that 'every one who exalts himself shall be humbled, and one who humbles himself shall be exalted.'[73]

O what wrong-headedness and distortion on the part of Adam's children! It is extremely difficult to ascend, but extremely easy to descend, yet they raise themselves with ease and lower themselves with difficulty; [they are] ready for the honors and heights of ecclesiastical offices that make even the shoulders of the angels tremble. Lord Jesus, scarcely are any found to follow you, who allow themselves to be drawn, or who are willingly led along the way of your commandments.[74] For some are drawn, and can say: 'Draw me after you.'[75] Others are led and say: 'The king has led me into his storerooms.'[76] Others are caught up as the Apostle was caught up to the third heaven.[77] Fortunate indeed are the first: in their patience they possess their souls.[78] Even more fortunate are the second, because they give praise to him[79] of their own will. Most fortunate of all are the third: as if having their power of free choice somehow buried in God's boundless mercy, they are caught up by a spirit of ardor[80] to the riches of his glory,[81] not knowing whether they are in or out of the body.[82]

Blessed is the one, Lord Jesus, whom you lead everywhere, [but] not that rebellious spirit who wanted to ascend at once and was struck by the full power of the divinity. As for us, your people and the sheep of your pasture,[83] may we follow you, through you, toward you, because you are the way, the truth, and the life:[84] the way in [your] example, the truth in [your] promise, in [your] reward the life. For you have the words of everlasting life; we recognize and believe[85] that you are the Christ, the Son of the living God, who are above all, God forever blessed.[86]

69. Mt 7:14   70. Ph 2:9   71. Lk 10:37
72. Eph 4:9   73. Lk 14:11, 18:14   74. Ps 118:32 (119:32)
75. Sg 1:4   76. Sg 1:4   77. 2 Co 12:2
78. Lk 21:19   79. Ps 27:7 (28:7)   80. Is 4:4
81. Rm 9:23; Eph 1:18   82. 2 Co 12:2   83. Ps 78:13 (79:13)
84. Jn 14:6   85. Jn 6:68-69   86. Rm 9:5

[the LORD'S ascension]

Sermon Three
THE UNDERSTANDING AND THE INCLINATION

TODAY THE LORD OF HEAVEN passed into the heights of heaven with heavenly power; dissipating the weaknesses of the flesh as if they were clouds, he put on a robe of glory.[1] High is the sun in its rising;[2] it has grown hot and gathered strength; its rays are far-reaching and multitudinous over the earth; and there is 'no one who can hide from its heat.'[3] The Wisdom of God[4] has returned to the land of wisdom where everyone both understands and seeks the good: their understanding is exceedingly acute, and their inclination is exceedingly intent 'on heeding the voice of his word.'[5]

We, however, are in this land where there is great wickedness and little wisdom, for 'the perishable body presses down the soul and the earthly dwelling burdens the mind that ponders many things.'[6] I think that 'mind' here means understanding, which is in fact pressed down when it ponders many things, when it does not gather itself together in the single exclusive meditation that takes its beginning from that city 'which is banded together in unity.'[7] This type of understanding must necessarily be pressed down and distracted by many things in many and diverse ways.[8] I think that [our] inclinations are called 'soul' here, for in a perishable body they are influenced by the different passions, which can never be mitigated, much less quieted, until the will seeks one thing and is directed toward one thing.

2. There are two parts of ourselves then, understanding and inclination, that must be purified: the understanding, that it may know; and the inclination, that it may will. Fortunate, truly fortunate, were those two men, Elijah and Enoch,[9] from whom every cause and occasion which might shackle either their understanding or inclination was removed. Living for God alone,[10] they know nothing but God and desire nothing but God.

1. Si 45:8/9. JB gives two verse numbers.
2. Jg 5:31
3. Ps 18:7 (19:6)
4. 1 Co 1:24
5. Ps 102:20 (103:20)
6. Ws 9:15
7. Ps 121:3 (122:3)
8. Heb 1:1
9. Gn 5:24
10. 1 Tm 1:17

We even read of Enoch 'that he was carried off, lest wickedness impair his understanding or deceit beguile his soul.'[11]

Our understanding was disordered, not to say blinded; [our] inclination was tainted, and very tainted. But Christ enlightens our understanding, [and] the Holy Spirit purifies our inclination. For the Son of God came. He worked so many great and wondrous deeds in the world, that with good cause he called our understanding away from all worldly matters. Thus we could ponder, and never have enough of pondering, that he has done wondrous deeds.[12] Truly he left very extensive fields for our discerning to roam, and the river of these ponderings is so very deep, that, in the words of the prophet, it cannot be crossed.[13] Who can sufficiently ponder how the Lord has come before us, come to us, come to our assistance; and how his unparalleled Majesty willed to die that we might live, to serve that we might reign, to live in exile that we might be brought home again, and even to stoop to the most menial actions so as to set us over[14] all his works.

3. The Lord of the apostles presented himself to the apostles in such a way that they would no longer perceive the invisible things of God as understood by the things that are made,[15] but that the very Maker of all things would himself be seen face to face.[16] Because the disciples were beings of flesh and God is spirit,[17] and spirit and flesh are not easily brought together, he adapted himself to them with the shadow of his body, that by the intervention of his life-giving flesh they might behold the Word in flesh,[18] the sun in a cloud, light in an earthen jug, the candle in the lantern. For 'the breath in our mouth [is] Christ the Lord, to whom we said: 'Under your shadow do we live among the nations.'[19] 'Under your shadow,' it says, 'among the nations'; not among the angels, where with purest eyes we shall behold the most pure light. Hence also the power of the Most High covered the Virgin with his shadow[20] lest even that peerless eagle be blinded by splendor beyond measure [and] be unable to endure divinity's lightning brightness.

11. Ws 4:11   12. Ps 97:1 (98:1)   13. Ezk 47:5
14. Gn 41:41   15. Rm 1:20   16. 1 Co 13:12
17. Jn 4:24   18. Jn 1:14   19. Lm 4:20
20. Lk 1:35

For this purpose [the Lord] set his flesh before them, to turn their every thought away from human matters and attach it to his flesh, which was saying wondrous things and performing wondrous deeds. Thus he would turn [their] attention from flesh to spirit, because 'God is spirit, and those who worship God must worship in spirit and in truth.'[21] Does it not seem to you that he enlightened their understanding when he opened their mind[s] to understanding of the Scriptures, making known that the Christ had to suffer these things and rise from the dead, and so enter into his glory?[22]

4. Still, having grown accustomed to that most holy flesh of his, they could not listen to a word about his departure: that the one for whom they had left everything[23] would leave them. What is the reason for this? [Their] understanding was enlightened, but [their] inclination was not yet purified. Whence their kind Teacher gently and tenderly addressed them, saying: 'It is for your good that I go. For if I do not go away, the Paraclete will not come to you.'[24] 'But because I have said these things to you, sorrow has filled your heart[s].'[25] What does it mean, that while Christ abides on earth, the Holy Spirit cannot come to them? Was [the Spirit] shrinking from any involvement with [Christ's] flesh? From the Spirit and by the Spirit was [Christ] conceived in the Virgin, and born from a virgin mother. It was nothing of the sort! [Christ] was showing us the path along which we were to walk, and putting before us the form with which we were to be impressed.

And as they wept,[26] Christ was lifted up to heaven.[27] He sent the Holy Spirit,[28] who purified their inclination, that is, their will; or rather he transformed it, so that those who at first wanted to detain the Lord, now preferred that he ascend. What he had foretold to them was fulfilled: 'You shall be sorrowful, but your sorrow will be turned into joy.'[29] In this way then, was their discerning enlightened by Christ, and [their] will purified by the Spirit, so that just as they knew the good, they would also will it. This only is perfect religion and religious perfection.

5. I now recall the saintly Elisha. He was told by Elijah to ask for whatever he wanted when the time came for the prophet's departure or ascension. His reply was: 'I pray that your spirit

21. Jn 4:24   22. Lk 24:25-27, 45-46   23. Mt 19:27
24. Jn 16:7   25. Jn 16:6   26. Jn 16: 20
27. Lk 24:51; Ac 1:9 28. Ac 2:2   29. Jn 16:20

may be twofold in me.' Elijah [answered]: 'You have requested
a difficult thing. And yet, if you see [me] when I am being taken
from you, what you have asked shall take place.'[30] Does it not
seem to you that Elijah represents the person of the ascending
Lord, and Elisha the group of apostles sighing anxiously at
Christ's ascension? For just as Elisha could not be torn away from
Elijah, so neither could the apostles be separated from the presence of Christ. He barely persuaded them at the end that it is
impossible to please God without faith.[31]

What then is the twofold spirit that is sought if not the enlight-
ening of the understanding and the purification of the inclination? [It is] 'a difficult thing' because one who deserves to have
it is rarely found on earth. 'And yet,' he says, 'if you see [me]
when I am being taken from you, what you have asked shall take
place.' Lord Jesus, your disciples need not and ought not to suffer any loss on this account, for as they were looking on, you
were lifted up into heaven,[32] and with wistful eyes they followed
you 'marching in the greatness of your strength.'[33] Surely we can
say that the twofold spirit [is] what the Saviour says to his disciples: 'One who believes in me will also perform the deeds that
I do, and greater than these will he do.'[34] Did not Peter perform
greater deeds than Christ, yet through Christ? We read that the
sick were laid in beds in the streets 'so that when Peter came by,
at least his shadow would be cast over some of them and they
would be freed from their infirmities.'[35] Now we never find that
the Lord cured infirmities with his shadow.

6. I do not doubt that the understanding of all of you who are
here present has been enlightened, but I am going to show with
evident logic that your inclination[s] have not been purified equally. All of you know what is good, the way on which to proceed,
and how you ought to proceed along it. But you do not have a
single will. For in all the exercises of this way and this life, some
not only walk but also run, or rather fly; so that to them their
vigils seem brief, their foods sweet,[36] their clothing soft, and their
labors not only bearable but even appealing. Others, however,
[are] not like this. Instead, with withered hearts and rebellious
dispositions, scarcely are they dragged to these [exercises];

30. 2 K 2:9-10   31. Heb 11:6   32. Ac 1:9
33. Is 63:1 and Jdt 16:5: *in multitudine fortitudinis suae* in the Vulgate.
34. Jn 14:12   35. Ac 5:15   36. Ps 54:15 (55:14)

scarcely are they compelled by fear of hell. Wretched and woe-begone, they share in [our] tribulation but not in [our] consolation. Is the hand of the Lord shortened[37] so that he cannot give to everyone when he opens his hand and fills every living creature with [his] blessing?[38] What then is the reason? Clearly it is this, that they do not see Christ when he is taken up from them; in other words, they do not ponder how he left them orphans,[39] that they are pilgrims and strangers[40] on earth, that as long as they are still held in the frightful prison of the filthy body, they cannot be with Christ.[41] Further, if people of this type have remained under a burden for a long time, they are overwhelmed and sink down, or else they are in a sort of hell, so that they never breathe fully in the light of the Lord's mercies[42] and in the Spirit's freedom, which alone makes [our] yoke easy and our burden light.[43]

7. The source of such a pernicious lukewarmness is that their inclination, that is, their will, has not yet been purified. Gravely diverted and allured by their own craving,[44] they do not choose the good as they know it. They are fond of little earthly consolations for their flesh, whether in word, or in sign, or in deed, or in anything else. If [they] sometimes take a break from these [things], they do not wholly break with [them]. Hence their inclinations are rarely directed toward God, and their compunction is not constant, but intermittent. Now a soul subject to these distractions cannot be satisfied with the Lord's visitations. The more it is emptied of the [distractions], the more fully will it be satisfied by the [visitations]. If [it is] greatly [emptied], [it will be] greatly [satisfied]; if [it is] barely [emptied], [it will be] barely [satisfied]. Surely, if you examine further, one can never be mixed with the other for all eternity. When the oil did not meet with an empty vessel, it had to stop flowing.[45] New wine is put only in new wineskins so that both may be preserved.[46] So, too, spirit and flesh,[47] fire and lukewarmness, do not abide in the same domicile, especially since lukewarmness is wont to provoke the Lord himself to vomit.[48]

37. Is 59:1
40. Gn 23:4; Lv 25:35
43. Mt 11:30
46. Mt 9:17

38. Ps 144:16 (145:16)
41. Ph 1:23
44. Jm 1:14
47. Ga 5:17

39. Jn 14:18
42. Si 36:1
45. 2 K 4:3,6
48. Rv 3:16

8. The apostles, who were still clinging to the Lord's flesh—uniquely holy because it belonged to the Saint of saints[49]— could not be filled with the Holy Spirit until it was taken away from them. Do you think that you, bound and inseparably glued to your flesh, which is very squalid and full of the images of every kind of impurity, can receive the perfectly pure and unadulterated Spirit if you have not tried to radically renounce those fleshly consolations? In fact, when you have begun sorrow will fill your heart;[50] but if you persevere, your sorrow will be turned into joy![51] For then [your] inclinations will be purified, and [your] will renewed, or rather created anew. Then through everything that at first seemed difficult, or even impossible, you will hasten with much pleasure and great eagerness.

'Send forth your Spirit,' [Scripture] says, 'and they will be created, and you will renew the face of the earth.'[52] Just as the outer person is recognized by the face, so the inner is represented by the will. When the Spirit has been sent, the face of the earth is created and renewed: this means that our earthly will becomes heavenly, ready at a nod to obey more quickly than a nod. Blessed are people like this, for not only do they perceive no evil, but they abide in a certain marvelous expansion of heart.[53] But concerning those we spoke of above, the Lord says these dreadful words: 'My spirit will not remain in those people, because they are flesh;'[54] that is, they are carnal, and whatever was spirit in them has passed away into the flesh.

9. Dearly beloved, today is the day when the Bridegroom is taken away from us,[55] and our minds are not without some disquiet. But it is for this purpose, that he may send us the Spirit of truth.[56] Let us weep and pray that the [Spirit] may find us or rather make us worthy,[57] and may fill this house where we are sitting[58] in order that not a violent shaking but his anointing may teach us everything.[59] Then when [our] understanding has been illuminated and [our] inclination purified, may he come to us and make his dwelling place in us.[60] Just as Moses' serpent swallowed up all the magicians' serpents,[61] so the [Spirit], when he comes,

49. Heb 9:2-3   50. Jn 16:6   51. Jn 16:20
52. Ps 103:30 (104:30)
53. Is 60:5: *et dilabitur cor tuum;* Ps 118:32 (119:32): *cum dilatastis cor meum.*
54. Gn 6:3   55. Mt 9:15   56. Jn 15:26
57. Ws 3:5   58. Ac 2:2   59. 1 Jn 2:27
60. Jn 14:23   61. Ex 7:12

will devour all fleshly consolations. Then will we have rest from labor, gladness from tribulation, and glory after abuse, just as those whom the Spirit filled 'went out from the council's presence rejoicing that they were considered worthy to suffer abuse for the sake of Jesus' name.'[62] The Spirit of Jesus, a good spirit,[63] a holy spirit,[64] an upright spirit,[65] a sweet spirit,[66] a ruling spirit,[67] makes light and broad whatever seems difficult and confining in this wicked world.[68] Disgrace he judges a joy, and contempt he persuades [us] is exaltation. 'Let us,' therefore, as the Prophet says, 'examine our ways' and our enthusiasms; 'let us lift up our hearts and [our] hands'[69] so that we may rejoice, and lavishly rejoice, on the solemn feast of the Holy Spirit, who leads us into all the truth,[70] just as the Son of God promised.

---

62. Ac 5:41   63. Lk 11:13   64. Ps 50:13 (51: 11)
65. Ps 50:12 (51:10)
66. Si 24: 20/27. JB gives 2 verse numbers, 20, and 27, as in the Vulgate, but it is memories that are sweet. Vulg: *spiritus enim meus super mel dulcis* (Si 24: 27).
67. Ps 50:14 (51:12)   68. Ga 1:4   69. Lm 3:40-41
70. Jn 16:13

[the LORD's ascension]

Sermon Four
THE VARIOUS WAYS OF ASCENDING

I F WE CELEBRATE THE SOLEMN FEASTS of the Lord's birth and resurrection with due devotion, it is appropriate that Ascension day be celebrated with no less devotion. In no way, of course, does this [feast] fall short of those feasts; it is rather their goal and fulfillment. Deservedly do we keep as a day of solemn feasting and gladness [that day] when the Sun above the heavens, the Sun of justice,[1] presented himself for us to look upon, and tempered his lightning brightness and unapproachable light[2] by a cloud of flesh and the sackcloth of mortality. Great too was the gladness and immense the exultation[3] when, stripped of the sackcloth, he was girded with gladness.[4] He did not indeed put aside the substance of his sackcloth, but its decrepitude, its decay, its misery and its worthlessness, [when] he consecrated the first fruits of our resurrection.

Nonetheless, what [do] these solemn feasts [mean] to me if my life[5] is still prolonged on earth? Would anyone have presumed even to yearn for an ascension to heaven if [Christ] who had descended does not ascend before us?[6] I tell you then that this place of exile would not seem to me more tolerable than hell if the Lord of Hosts had not left us a seed[7] of confidence and expectation when he was lifted up on the clouds[8] and gave hope to believers! 'Unless I go away,' he says, 'the Paraclete will not come to you.'[9] What Paraclete? Assuredly the one through whom love is poured out and hope no longer disappoints [us];[10] that Paraclete through whom our life is in heaven,[11] the Power from on high,[12] [the one] through whom our hearts are lifted up. 'I go to prepare a place for you,' he says; 'and if I depart, I will come again, and I will take you to myself.'[13] 'Wherever the body is, there will the eagles be gathered.'[14] Do you not see how the solemn feast we celebrate today is the fulfillment of the other

---

1. Ml 4:2
2. 1 Tm 6:16
3. Ps 44:16 (45:15)
4. Ps 29:12 (30:11)
5. Ph 3:20
6. Eph 4:9-10
7. Rm 9:29
8. Ac 1:9
9. Jn 16: 7
10. Rm 5:5
11. Ph 3:20
12. Lk 24:49
13. Jn 14:2-3
14. Mt 24:28

solemn feasts, how it manifests their consequences, and increases their grace?

2. Just like everything else pertaining to the one who was born for us and given to us,[15] so too his ascension was accomplished on our behalf, and works for us. In our lives, many things happen[16] by chance and many out of necessity. But Christ, the power of God and the wisdom of God,[17] could not be subject to either. For what necessity could constrain the power of God, or what could the wisdom of God do by chance? Accordingly, do not doubt that whatever he said, whatever he performed, whatever he suffered was deliberate, filled with hidden meanings, filled with salvation. Since we know these things, if we should at some time happen to learn any one of them which comes from Christ, we ought to attend to it not as if we are bringing forward a sort of improvisation, but as something which would not have happened without some reason, even if we do not know it beforehand. For just as a writer arranges everything for specific reasons, so the things that are from God are appointed;[18] and especially those performed by [his] majesty present in the flesh.

But alas! how limited our discernment, and how impoverished our knowledge! We discern only in part,[19] and what a meagre part! Scarcely do little flickers shine on us from so radiant a light-source—from the lamp placed on the lamp-stand.[20] Inasmuch as each of us receives little, the things revealed to one must be more faithfully imparted to the others. For my part, brothers, I have neither the wish, nor the right to keep from you anything he himself has deigned to grant me for your edification[21] about his ascension, or rather about his ascensions, especially since this is the special prerogative of spiritual gifts, that when imparted they are not diminished. Perhaps these things are known to some of you to whom they were revealed as they were to me; but it is incumbent on me to speak of what I perceive, because of some who might by chance not notice, being intent on more sublime matters and occupied with other things; and also because of those who are less capable of understanding.

3. 'Christ who descended is the very one who also ascended.'[22] These are the words of the Apostle. And I myself believe that

---

15. Is 9:6   16. MSS. P and S read *fiunt*.   17. 1 Co 1:24
18. Rm 13:1   19. 1 Co 13:12   20. Mt 5:15
21. 2 Co 12: 19   22. Eph 4:10

he ascended in this very act of descending, for it was necessary that Christ[23] descend in order that we might be taught to ascend. Surely we are all eager for ascent; we all crave exaltation. We are noble creatures, and [have] greatness of soul; for that reason, we have a natural urge to long for the heights.

But woe to us if we should want to follow him who said: 'I shall take my seat on the mountain of the covenant, on the northern slopes.'[24] Alas, wretch, 'on the northern slopes!' That mountain is very cold; we do not follow you. You have a craving for power, and you dream of the heights of influence. How many, even today, follow [your] foul and unfortunate footsteps! Yes, and how few escape, and are not dominated by the lust to dominate! That is why those who hold authority are called benefactors;[25] that is why 'the sinner glories in the desires of his soul.'[26] Assuredly, all flatter the powerful; all envy [them]. Whom do you follow, you wretched humans, whom do you follow? Do you not see Satan, falling like lightning?[27] Is this not the mountain which an angel ascended and became a devil?[28] Be mindful that after his fall [he was] tortured with envy and evilly preoccupied with casting down humankind; yet in no way did he dare to urge the ascent of that mountain on which he would surely be recognized as one known for his faulty ascent as much as for his appalling fall.

4. Yet the crafty foe was not at a loss what to do. He showed humankind another, similar mountain, saying: 'You will be like gods, knowing good and evil.'[29] This ascent too is ruinous; rather it is a descent, greater than [the one] from Jerusalem to Jericho.[30] Knowledge that puffs up[31] is a most evil mountain; yet even today you see many of the children of Adam creeping up it with urgent craving, as if they did not know how far their father descended by his ascent of that mountain, or rather how grievously he fell, [and] the extent to which his entire posterity was completely cast down and shattered. The wounds inflicted on you by that ascent of the mountain have not yet been healed, even though you were still lying hidden in your father. Are you now

---

23. Lk 24:46
24. Is 14:13. Cf. Gregory the Great, *Hom. Ezech.*, 1; PL 76: 798-800.
25. Lk 22:25   26. Ps 9:24 (10:3)   27. Lk 10:18
28. Is 14:12-14   29. Gn 3:5   30. Lk 10:30
31. 1 Co 8:1

attempting to ascend it again in your own person, so that the last mistake will be worse than the first?[32]

What craving is so cruel for you wretched people? 'Children of humanity, how long [will you be] heavy in heart? Why do you love vanity and seek falsehood?'[33] Do you not know that God chooses what is weak in the world to confound the strong, and what is foolish in the world to confound the wise?[34] The fear of divine threat does not call us back— [the threat that] he will destroy the wisdom of the wise and bring to nothing the prudence of the prudent.[35] Neither does the example of [our] father [Adam call us back], nor our own good sense and the experience of harsh necessity to which we have been handed over by our senseless appetite for knowledge.

5. See, brothers, we have shown you the other mountain, not for you to ascend, but for you to flee. It is the very [mountain] he was ascending who wanted to be like God and to have knowledge of good and evil,[36] the very [mountain] his children are even today heaping up and piling high. They find nothing too worthless to use in raising up a mountain of knowledge. You may see one person eagerly striving after culture, another after the management of secular matters, this one trying for the pleasing expression of opinions which are displeasing to God, and that one attempting some common trade. So intensely does each pursue knowledge that he does not consider it work if only he can be considered more learned than others. In this way they build up Babel,[37] and think that they will attain likeness to God.[38] In this way they crave what is not for their good and neglect what is.

What do these mountains mean to you, [when] they are so difficult and so dangerous to ascend? Why do you forsake the mountain whose ascent is both easy and very useful? The ambition for power deprived the angel [Satan] of angelic bliss; his appetite for knowledge despoiled the human of the glory of immortality. Let someone attempt to climb the mountain of power—how many opponents do you think he will have? How many will he find to drive him back? How many obstacles? How difficult a path? What if it should happen that at last he obtains what he desired? Scripture says, 'The mighty shall be mightily tormented,'[39] and

32. Mt 27:64   33. Ps 4:3 (4:2)   34. 1 Co 1:27
35. 1 Co 1:19   36. Gn 3:5   37. Gn 11:4-9
38. Gn 1:26   39. Ws 6:7

so I shall not mention the present concerns and anxieties that power itself produces. Another person is greedy for the knowledge [that] puffs up.[40] How greatly will he toil, how anxious will his spirit be?[41] And still he may hear: 'Not even if you burst yourself . . . .'[42] His eye will be fixed in bitterness[43] as often as he happens to see anyone to whom he judges himself inferior, or thinks that others do. What if he should greatly swell up [with his knowledge]? The Lord says: 'I will destroy the wisdom of the wise and bring to nothing the prudence of the prudent.'[44]

6. Now I would not prolong this unduly. I think you have seen that we must flee each of these mountains if we are really terrified of the angel's headlong plunge, [and] the human's fall. 'Mountains of Gilboa, let no dew or rain come upon you.'[45] Yet what are we doing? It is not expedient to ascend in this way, yet we are seized with the craving to ascend.

Who will teach us a salutary ascent? Who but the one of whom we read that 'he who descended is the very one who ascended'?[46] He was the one who had to show us a way of ascent so that we would not follow either the footsteps or advice of the wicked leader, or rather misleader. Because he found nowhere he could ascend, the Most High descended, and by his descent he prepared for us a satisfying and salutary ascent. He descended from the mountain[47] of power, clothed in the frailty of the flesh;[48] he descended from the mountain of knowledge, because 'it pleased God to save believers through the folly of what is preached.'[49] What appears weaker than the delicate body and limbs of a child? What looks less learned than a little one who knows only [its] mother's breast? Who [is] more powerless than one whose every limb was fastened with nails,[50] whose bones were counted?[51] Who appears more senseless than the one who delivered his soul to death,[52] and then restored what he had not stolen?[53] You see how far he descended, how greatly he emptied himself of his

---

40. 1 Co 8:1   41. Ps. 142:4 (143:4)
42. Horace, Satires, 2, 3, 319 *(non, si te ruperis, par eris)* A young frog was trying to let his mother know how big was the calf whose foot crushed his brothers and sisters. The mother frog swelled up and asked, 'This big' . . . The young frog told her, 'Though you burst yourself, you'll never be as big'.
43. Jb 17:2   44. 1 Co 1:19   45. 2 S 1:21
46. Eph 4:10   47. Ex 19:14, Mt 8:1   48. Rm 6:19; Gal 4:13; Heb 5:2
49. 1 Co 1:21   50. Jn 20:25   51. Ps 21:18 (22:17)
52. Is 53:12   53. Ps 68:5 (69:4)

own power and wisdom![54] Yet he could not have climbed any higher up the mountain of goodness, nor found a clearer way of commending his love.[55] Nor is it astonishing that Christ ascended by descending, when both of the former fell by ascending. And it seems to me that it was the one ascending this mountain who was sought [by the psalmist] who asked: 'Who will ascend the mountain of the Lord, and who will stand in his holy place?'[56] Perhaps even Isaiah, seeing people falling from their desire to ascend, was calling them to this mountain when he exclaimed: 'Come, let us ascend the mountain of the Lord!'[57] Is [the psalmist] not manifestly charging them with ascending the former mountains [of knowledge and power] when he affirms the luxuriance of this mountain, saying, 'Why look enviously upon the rugged mountains? [Here is] a rugged mountain, a fruitful mountain.'[58] This is then the 'mountain of the Lord's house, established on the highest of the mountains,'[59] where the bridegroom was beheld leaping by the one who said: ' Behold, he comes, leaping on the mountains!'[60] He was teaching one unacquainted with the way, drawing a little child along, leading forth an infant. For that reason he was going step by step, as it were, so that from strength to strength the God of gods might be seen on Zion.[61] For his justice is like the mountains of God.[62]

7. If you wish, let us now consider those leaps too with which like a giant he exulted to run his course, whose rising is from highest heaven; he runs step by step even to its height.[63] Imagine first the mountain he ascended with Peter, James and John,[64] where 'he was transfigured before them. His face shone like the sun, and his clothing became white as the snow.'[65] This is the glory of the resurrection which we contemplate on the mountain of hope. Why did he ascend to be transfigured if not to teach us to ascend by pondering that 'future glory which will be revealed in us'?[66]

Fortunate is the one whose meditation is always in the Lord's sight,[67] who with unremitting pondering turns over in his heart the delights of the Lord's right hand for evermore![68] What can seem burdensome to one who is always calling to mind that the

54. Ph 2:7
55. Rm 5:8
56. Ps 23:3 (24:3)
57. Is 2:3; Mi 4:2
58. Ps 67:17 (68:16)
59. Is 2: 2; Mi 4:1
60. Sg 2:8
61. Ps 83:8 (84:7)
62. Ps 35:7 (36:6)
63. Ps 18:6-7 (19: 5-6)
64. Mt 17:1
65. Mt 17:2
66. Rm 8:18
67. Ps 18:15 (19:14)
68. Ps 15:11 (16:11)

sufferings of this age are not worth comparing to the future glory?[69] What can anyone crave in [this] evil age[70] whose eye is always[71] seeing the good things of the Lord in the land of the living,[72] always seeing the everlasting rewards? 'To you my heart has spoken'—the prophet is talking to the Lord—'to you my heart has spoken: my face has searched for you; your face, Lord, will I continue to seek.'[73] Who can grant me[74] that all of you rising up should stand on high[75] and see the exultation which will come to you from the Lord?[76]

8. Do not be annoyed, I beg you, if we linger on this mountain a while longer, for we will be able to pass over the others more quickly. In fact, who would not be held on this [mountain] by blessed Peter's utterance, when he spoke on it and about it, saying: 'Lord, it is good for us to be here'?[77] For what is as good, or what else ever seems good, as for a soul to live in good things,[78] since the body still cannot. I think that [Peter's words], 'it is good for us to be here,' came from one who was entering 'the place of the wondrous tabernacle up to the very house of God, with cries of rejoicing and praise, the sound of a feasting throng.'[79] Now who among you inwardly pondering that future life, the gladness, the joyousness, the happiness, the glory of God's children,[80] who, I say, turning such things over in a conscience at peace with itself, does not immediately utter out of a fullness of inner pleasure : 'Lord, it is good for us to be here'? Clearly not in this pilgrimage full of suffering, where he is held back in the body, but in that pleasant and salutary pondering wherein his heart enables him to live. 'Who will give me wings like a dove's, and I will fly away and find rest!'[81] Yet you, children of humanity, children of the man who descended from Jersualem to Jericho,[82] 'children of humanity, how long will you be heavy in heart?'[83] Ascend to a high heart, and God will be exalted,[84] for this is the mountain on which Christ is transfigured. Ascend, and you will know that the Lord has dealt wondrously with his Holy one.[85]

69. Rm 8:18
70. Ga 1:4
71. Ps. 24:15 (25:15)
72. Ps 26:13 (27:13)
73. Ps 26:8 (27:8)
74. Jb 19:23
75. Ba 5:5
76. Ba 4:36
77. Mt 17:4
78. Ps 24:13 (25:13)
79. Ps 41:5 (42:4)
80. Rm 5:2, 8:21
81. Ps 54:7 (55:6)
82. Lk 10:30
83. Ps 4:3 (4:2)
84. Ps 63:7-8 (64:6)
85. Ps 4:4 (4:3)

9. I beseech you, my brothers,[86] do not let your hearts be weighed down with worldly concerns.[87] Thanks [be to] God, I do not find it particularly necessary to admonish you about dissipation and drunkedness.[88] Disburden your hearts, I beseech you, of the weighty mass of earthly ponderings, that you may know the Holy one with whom the Lord has dealt wondrously.[89] Lift up your hearts with the hands[90] of [your] ponderings, that you may see the transfigured Lord. Prepare in your hearts not only the tents of the patriarchs and prophets, but all the diverse mansions of that heavenly home,[91] like the one who went about in the Lord's tent, offering a sacrifice of jubilation,[92] singing and reciting this song to the Lord: 'How beloved [are] your tabernacles, O Lord of Hosts! My soul longs and faints for the courts of the Lord!'[93]

You too, dearly beloved, must go about with a sacrifice of loyalty and devotion, visiting with [your] mind the heavenly habitations, and the many dwelling places which are in [our] Father's house;[94] humbly casting down your hearts before the throne of God and the Lamb;[95] reverently supplicating each of the orders of angels, [and] greeting the body of patriarchs, the group of prophets, and the assembly of apostles; acknowledging the martyrs' crowns resplendent with purple flowers; marveling at the choirs of virgins, fragrant with the scent of lilies; turning your ears, as much as your weak heart allows, to the honeyed sound of a new song.[96]

'I remembered these things,' the prophet says, 'and I poured out my soul within me.' What things? 'How I went into the place of the wondrous tabernacle, to the very house of God.'[97] And again, 'I remembered God, and I found delight.'[98] This man saw the one whom the apostles saw, and I think [it was] a vision not unlike that of the apostles, except that his vision was completely spiritual, with nothing physical about it. Certainly [the prophet] did not see him as did the one who said: 'We saw him and there was no beauty or comeliness in him.'[99] There is no doubt that he saw him transfigured and more beautiful in appearance than

86. Rm 12:1, 15:30   87. Lk 21:34   88. Lk 21:34
89. Ps 4:4 (4:3)   90. Lm 3:41   91. Jn 14:2
92. Ps 26:6 (27:6)   93. Ps 83:2-3 (84:1-2)   94. Jn 14:2
95. Rv 4:10, 8:3, 14:4   96. Rv 14:3   97. Ps 41:5 (42:4)
98. Ps 76:4 (77:3)   99. Is 53:2

the children of humanity;[100] he shows his delight just like the apostles who say: 'It is good for us to be here!'[101] And that nothing may be lacking to the similarity set forth, we read that [the apostles] fell prostrate,[102] while [the prophet] admits that his spirit grew faint.[102]

'How great is the abundance of your sweetness, Lord, that you have reserved for those who fear you!'[104] Ascending this mountain, [my brothers,] and 'gazing on the glory of the Lord with unveiled faces,'[105] certainly you too will have to cry out: 'Draw us after you!'[106] Of what advantage is it to know where you ought to go, if you are not familiar with the way to go?

10. Accordingly, you must ascend a second mountain. On this one you can hear [Christ] preaching and setting up a ladder fitted with eight rungs, its top touching heaven.[107] 'Blessed are those who suffer persecution because of justice, for theirs is the kingdom of heaven.'[108] Now if you ascended the first mountain by continual meditation on celestial glory, you will not find it a heavy burden to ascend this mountain, in order to meditate on his law day and night,[109] just as this very prophet used to meditate not only on the rewards but also on the Lord's commandments, which he loved.[110] So you too will hear: 'And where I am going, you know,'[111] on account of the first ascension; 'and you know the way,'[112] on account of the second. For that reason, set your heart on[113] searching for the way of truth,[114] lest perhaps you be among the number of those who 'have not found the way to a city to dwell in.'[115] Instead, be concerned to ascend, not only by pondering heavenly glory, but also by living in a way that merits heavenly glory.

11. I read no less of a third mountain on which [Christ] ascends alone to pray.[116] You see then how aptly the bride in the Song says: 'Behold, he comes, leaping on the mountains!'[117] On the first [mountain] he was transfigured,[118] so that you might know where to direct yourself; on the second he spoke the words of

100. Ps 44:3 (45:2)   101. Mt. 17:4   102. Mt 17:6
103. Ps 76:4 (77:3); Ps 141:4 (142:3)
104. Ps 30:20 (31:19)   105. 2 Co 3:18   106. Sg 1:4
107. Gn 28:12   108. Mt 5:10   109. Ps 1:2
110. Ps 118:47 (119:47)   111. Jn 14:4   112. Jn 14:4
113. Jb 22:22   114. Ps 118:30 (119:30) 115. Ps 106:4 (107:4)
116. Mt 14:23   117. Sg 2:8   118. Mt 17:2

life,[119] so that you might know how to reach these; he prayed on the third,[120] so that you might strive to obtain the right disposition for journeying and for reaching [your destination]. 'It is a sin for anyone to know good and not do it.'[121] Therefore, since you know that the right disposition is given in prayer, when you see what has to be done, you too, ascend to pray in order to gain the strength for doing what you see. Pray earnestly, pray persistently, just as [Christ] used to spend the whole night in prayer,[122] and the good Father will give the good Spirit to the one who is asking him.[123] And see how it is to our benefit, at the time of prayer, even to seek a place of physical seclusion. [Christ] taught this not only in word, when he said: 'Go into your own room, and with the door closed, pray to your Father,'[124] but also recommended it with [his] example, not allowing any of his friends to come, but ascending alone to pray.

12.   Do you think we will be able to find anything further about his ascensions? Of course, we will. For I do not want you to be unmindful of the beast of burden onto which we read that he ascended.[125] Nor do I want you to leave out the ascent of the cross, for it was necessary that the 'Son of man' be lifted up on it too.[126] 'When I have been lifted up from the earth,' he says, 'I will draw all things to myself.'[127]

And so what will you do when knowledge is present, and will is added to it, but you find you cannot accomplish what is good; when ass-like and bestial impulses possess a conflicting law and want to hold you prisoner?[128] What, I say, do you do about the irrational cravings that are in the parts of your body? When you decide to fast, the lure of gluttony besets you; when you are bent on keeping a vigil, drowsiness bears down upon you. What do we do with this ass [of ours]? For this is ass-like, something we have in common with asses, for [the human being] 'has been matched with senseless beasts, and has become like them.'[129] Ascend on to this ass, Lord; trample down these bestial impulses, for they must be dominated, lest they prevail and have dominion [over us]. Unless they are trampled down, they will tread us under foot; unless they are repressed, they will oppress us. My

---

119. Mt 5:1-2; Jn 6:69
120. Mt 14:23
121. Jm 4:17
122. Lk 6:12
123. Lk 11:3
124. Mt 6:6
125. Mt 21:2-7
126. Lk 24:7, 46
127. Jn 12:32
128. Rm 7:23
129. Ps 48:13 (49:12); cf. Qo 3:18-19

soul, follow Christ the Lord in this ascension too, so that desire may be subject to you, and you may have dominion over it.[130] For you to ascend to heaven, you must first lift yourself above yourself[131] by treading upon the carnal passions that wage war against[132] you from within you.

13. Follow Christ also as he ascends the cross, [and] is lifted up from earth,[133] that you may position yourself not only above yourself, but above the entire world too, on the summit of the mind, looking down at all the things that are on earth,[134] and looking down upon them [too], as it was written: 'They will behold a land from afar.'[135] Let no pleasures of the world influence you, no adversities cast [you] down. Far be it from you to glory except in the cross of your Lord Jesus Christ, through whom the world has been crucified to you,[136] so that what the world covets, you will view as a cross; and [through whom] you have been crucified to the world, so that what the world views as a cross, you will embrace in the fullness of love.

14. Now what remains but for you to ascend to him 'who is above all, God forever blessed!'[137] To depart and be with Christ [is] by far the best thing.[138] 'Blessed is the man whose help is from you,' says the prophet to the Lord; 'in his heart he has disposed his ascents;'[139] he will go from strength to strength until he sees the God of gods in Zion.[140] This is the last ascension, in which everything finds fulfillment. As the Apostle says: 'Christ who descended is the very one who ascended, that he might bring all things to fulfillment.'[141] But what shall I say of that ascension? Where will we ascend in order that where Christ is, there we too may be?[142] What will it be like there? No eye has seen, apart from you, O God, what you have prepared for those who love you![143] Let us long for this [ascension], my brothers, let us aspire to it continually. Let the love in our hearts be strengthened in the measure that our understanding fails.

130. Gn 4:7
131. Lm 3:28
132. 1 P 2:11
133. Jn 12:32
134. Col 1:20
135. Is 33:17
136. Ga 6:14
137. Rm 9:5
138. Ph 1:23
139. Ps 83:6 (84:5)
140. Ps 83:8 (84:7)
141. Eph 4:10
142. Col 3:1; Jn 14:3
143. 1 Co 2:9

[the LORD's ASCENSION]

Sermon Five
COURAGE, FORBEARANCE, AND CONCORD

Saint Luke briefly commends to us the threefold [manifestation of] virtue in the early Church when he describes how, after the Lord's ascension, they 'steadfastly continued to pray with concord,'[1] awaiting the heavenly consolation they had been promised.[2] Indeed, with praiseworthy courage the little flock,[3] deprived of their Shepherd's support, but not doubting that he would care for them[4] and would show a parent's concern for them, knocked on heaven's gate with ardent supplications, certain that the prayer of the just would pierce[5] it, and that the prayers of the poor would not be spurned by the Lord,[6] nor return without [his] abundant blessing. With great forbearance they persisted without growing weak in accord with the prophet's saying: 'If he seems slow, wait for him because he will come and will not delay.'[7] And concord is clearly meant in what we read, because this [virtue] alone merits the gifts of the divine Spirit. 'For God is not [a God] of dissension but of peace,'[8] and does not make [anyone] dwell in a home unless there is harmony.[9]

2. Rightly then did the divine ear 'hear the readiness of their hearts,'[10] and not disappoint the expectations[11] of those who possessed courage, forbearance, and concord, for these are perfectly sure signs of faith, hope, and charity. Clearly hope brings about forbearance, and charity concord; but does faith bring about courage? It does, [faith] alone. If anything is rashly undertaken, without faith, there is no firm resoluteness of soul but instead a windy puffing-up and worthless swelling. Will you hear a person of courage? 'I can [do] all things,' [Paul] says, 'in the one who gives me strength.'[12]

Brothers, if we are longing to obtain the Spirit in the measure that runs over,[13] let us imitate this threefold readiness. The Spirit is given with reserve[14] to everyone except Christ, yet the abun-

1. Ac 1:14 2. Ac 1:4, 9:31 3. Lk 12:32
4. 1 P 5:7 5. Si 35:17/21 6. Ps 21:25 (22:24)
7. Hab 2:3, used in the antiphon *Ecce apparebit* for the Second Sunday of Advent.
8. 1 Co 14:33 9. Ps 67:7 (68:6) 10. Ps 9:38 (10:17)
11. Ps 118:16 (119:116) 12. Ph 4:13 13. Lk 6:38
14. Jn 3:34

dance of the measure that runs over seems somehow to exceed [all] measure. Courage was evident in our conversion; may forbearance be manifest at [our] end, and concord in our way of life. The heavenly Jerusalem[15] truly calls out to be built by people like this, who because of faith do not lack the greatness to take on Christ's burden, whose perseverance shows the extent of their hope, and who are joined together in charity 'which is the bond of perfection.'[16]

15. Heb 12:22   16. Col 3:14

[the lord's ascension]

Sermon Six
THE UNDERSTANDING AND THE INCLINATION

TODAY THE 'SON OF MAN' was brought before[1] the Ancient of days, sitting on his throne,[2] to be seated as an equal with him. From now on not only will he be 'the branch of the Lord in splendor and glory,' but also 'the sublime fruit of the earth.'[3] [This is] a blessed union and a mystery to be embraced with unutterable joy! For the 'branch of the Lord' and the 'fruit of the earth' are one and the same; the very Son of God[4] and the fruit of Mary's womb[5] are one and the same; David's son and Lord are one and the same,[6] who today completes the joy of him[7] who long ago sang in prophecy: 'The Lord said to my Lord: Sit at my right hand.'[8] How could the 'branch of the Lord' not be [David's] Lord? Yet [he is] also [David's] son, since he is 'the sublime fruit of the earth,' the fruit of the stalk which came forth from Jesse's root.[9]

Today, therefore, the Father glorifies at his side his Son, [who is] also the Son of humankind,[10] with the glory [the Son] had with [the Father] before the world was made.[11] Today heaven takes pride in having returned to it the Truth which has sprung up from the earth.[12] Today the Bridegroom is taken away from [his] friends and they must mourn, just as he himself foretold. For the friends of the Bridegroom could not mourn while the Bridegroom was with them, but the day has come for him to be taken from them, and from now on they will mourn and fast.[13] Peter, where are those words of yours now: 'Lord, it is good for us to be here; let us make here three tents'?[14] Behold, [Christ] has entered the 'greater and more perfect tent, not made by hands, that is, not belonging to this creation.'[15]

2. How then is it still 'good for us to be here'? Rather, it is grievous; it is burdensome; it is perilous. Surely so, where an abundance of wickedness is found, but little wisdom, if any at all;

---

1. Heb 9:28
2. Rv 5:13; Dn 7:9
3. Is 4:2
4. Mt 4:3
5. Lk 1:42
6. Mt 22:45
7. Jn 3:29
8. Ps 109:1 (110:1); Mt 22:44
9. Is 11:1
10. Mt 8:20
11. Jn 17:5
12. Ps 84:12 (85:11)
13. Mt 9:15
14. Mt 17:4
15. Heb 9:11

57

where everything is sticky, everything is slippery, shrouded in darkness[16] [and] surrounded with sinners' snares; where souls are imperiled and spirits are disheartened; here, under the sun, where there is only 'vanity and vexation of spirit.'[17]

My brothers, let us then lift up, let us lift up our hearts to heaven, along with our hands,[18] and let us strain to follow our ascending Lord with steps, so to speak, of commitment and faith. [A time] will come when, without delay [and] without difficulty, we will be caught up in the clouds to meet him;[19] then [our] spiritual bodies[20] will be able to achieve what now our physical spirits rightly cannot. For how much effort is now needed to lift up [our] hearts when—as lamentably enough we read in the book of [our] own experience—the perishable body burdens and the earthly dwelling presses down.[21]

3. Perhaps instruction is needed about what it means to lift up the heart,[22] and how it is to be raised up; but instruction by the Apostle rather than by us. 'Since you have risen in company with Christ' he says, 'seek the things that are above, where Christ is, seated at God's right hand; savor the things above, not those on the earth.'[23] It is as if he were to say more plainly: 'Since you have risen in his company,' ascend with [him] too; since you live with him, reign with him too.[24] Let us follow, brothers, let us follow the Lamb wherever he goes.[25] Let us follow him when he suffers; let us also follow him when he rises; and let us follow him even more joyfully when he ascends. Let our former self be crucified together with him, so that the sinful body may be destroyed, and we may no longer be slaves to sin,[26] since the parts of ourselves that are on earth have been put to death.[27] Then too, as he was raised from the dead by the glory of the Father, so we too may walk in newness of life.[28] For he died and rose for this purpose,[29] 'that we, having died to sin, might live to righteousness.'[30]

4. Furthermore, because newness of life[31] requires a place of greater safety and the dignity of resurrection calls for a loftier position, let us follow him even as he ascends, which means to

16. Ws 19:16	17. Qo 1:14	18. Lm 3:41
19. 1 Th 4:17	20. 1 Co 15:44	21. Ws 9:15
22. Lm 3:41	23. Col 3:1-2	24. 2 Tm 2:11-12
25. Rv 14:4	26. Rm 6:6	27. Col 3:5
28. Rm 6:4	29. Rm 14:9	30. 1 P 2:24
31. Rm 6:4		

seek and savor the things that are above, where he is, not those on the earth.[32] Do you ask what that place might be? Hear the Apostle speaking: 'It is the Jerusalem on high which is free; she is our mother.'[33] Do you want to know what things are there? It is a vision of peace:[34] 'Praise the Lord, Jerusalem, Zion, praise your God;'[35] 'he has established peace in your borders.'[36] O peace that surpasses all understanding![37] O peace even beyond peace! O measure beyond measure, pressed down, and shaken together, and running over![38] Suffer then with Christ,[39] christian soul; rise with him, ascend with him. This is [what the psalmist says]: 'Turn away from evil and do good; seek peace and pursue it.'[40] Surely Paul, as is recorded in the Acts of the Apostles, taught his followers in this way about abstinence and righteousness[41] and the hope of eternal life.[42] Truth itself in the gospel exhorts us to gird our loins, to light our lamps, and be found thereafter like people waiting for their master.[43]

5. Finally, if you paid careful attention, the ascension that the Apostle recommends to us is twofold, in that he admonished [us] both to seek and to savor, not the lowest things, but those on high. Perhaps it will be seen that the prophet, too, did not completely pass over this distinction when he said: 'Seek peace and pursue it.'[44] Thus seeking the peace we are to pursue, [and] pursuing [the peace] that has been sought, would be the same as seeking what is to be savored, [and] savoring what we have sought: [namely,] the things that are above and not the things on earth.[45] Assuredly, as long as our hearts are divided and found to have many recesses, and do not appear at all consistent with themselves, we must lift them up piecemeal and somehow part by part. The purpose is they may be brought together in that celestial Jerusalem [46] 'which is banded together in unity,'[47] where not only individuals but all alike begin to dwell together as one,[48] undivided not only within themselves, but undivided also among themselves.[49]

32. Col 3:1-2   33. Ga 4:26
34. See the 6-7th century hymn for the Office of the Dedication of a Church *Urbs beata Jerusalem / dicta pacis visio...*; CLS 2: 232-233.
35. Ps 147:12   36. Ps 147:14   37. Ph 4:7
38. Lk 6:38   39. Rm 8:17
40. Ps 33:15 (34:14); 36:27 (37:27); RB Prol. 17
41. Ac 24:25   42. Tt 1:2; 3:7   43. Lk 12:35-36
44. Ps 33:15 (34:14)   45. Col 3:1-2   46. Ga 4:26
47. Ps 121:3 (122:3)   48. Ps 132:1 (133:1)   49. Lk 11:17

Notice then, as I distinguish the principal parts of the heart itself, that there is understanding in us, and inclination, too, and they often act in opposition to one another.[50] One seems to look for the highest things, the other to long for the lowest. We can gather how truly great [is] the pain, how grievous the soul's torment, when it is so torn, so wounded, so divided from itself; at least from this that everyone experiences publicly, the dividing of a body—even if anyone has failed to heed it within his own spirit because of his destructive and dangerous lack of attention. The legs of a person [in the stocks] are pulled apart and the feet forced away from each other by a rather long block of wood; and even if the skin still remains whole, yet what must that torment be?

6. We lament that wretched people are thus afflicted, those who live among us in the body, perhaps enlightened like us, but who are not found to share our dispositions. They have an understanding of the good they do equal to ours, but not an equal love of what they understand. Now what excuse for ignorance do we [have], brothers, we who are never without religious instruction, never without sacred reading, never without spiritual learning? 'Whatever things are true and chaste, whatever are just and worthy of love, whatever things are of good repute, and if [there be] virtue and praise of discipline: these you have learned and accepted, and likewise you have heard and seen'[51] in the examples and words of those among you who are spiritually mature, whose encouragement and way of life so fully instruct all [of you]. If only these things, as they arouse our understanding, would also influence our inclination! Then there would be within us no exceedingly bitter contradiction, no divided state so difficult to endure, when from the one side we are drawn upward, and from the other dragged back down again!

7. Truly you can observe in nearly all religious communities men filled with consolation [and] overflowing with great joy.[52] [They are] always pleasant and cheerful; fervent in spirit,[53] they meditate day and night on God's law,[54] repeatedly looking up to heaven[55] and lifting up blameless hand[s] in prayer.[56] They carefully watch over [their] consciences and are dedicated to the

50. Ga 5:17   51. Ph 4:8-9   52. 2 Co 7:4
53. Rm 12:11   54. Ps 1:2   55. Mk 7:34
56. 1 Tm 2:8

pursuit of good deeds.[57] To them discipline seems worthy of love, fasting sweet, vigils brief, and manual labor pleasant. In sum, every austerity in this way of life seems invigorating to them.

On the other hand, clearly we encounter people [who are] irresolute and lax, who lose heart when burdened, who are in need of rod and spurs. Their gladness is listless, [and] their grief irresolute. For them compunction [is] fleeting and infrequent, [their] pondering sense-bound, their way of life lukewarm, their obedience lacking dedication, their speech imprudent, their prayer lacking the heart's intention,[58] and their reading without edification. Indeed, we see that the fear of hell barely restrains them, [and] shame barely contains them. Reason barely bridles them, and monastic observance barely confines them.

Is it not apparent to you that the life of these people approaches the borders of hell,[59] as their understanding fights with their inclination, and their inclination with their understanding? They are obliged to undertake[60] the deeds of the strong without being in the least sustained by the food of the strong; clearly they share [our] tribulation, but not [our] consolation.[61] I speak to whoever is like this among us: let us stand up and restore [our] souls, let us recollect [our] spirits and cast off pernicious lukewarmness, not only because it is perilous and is wont to cause God to vomit,[62] as from time to time we wretchedly lament, but because it is certainly very difficult to endure, full of misery and pain, in plain proximity to hell, [and is] the shadow of death.[63]

8. If we are seeking the things above,[64] let us strive in the meantime to savor and taste them in advance. Perhaps our being admonished both to seek and to savor the things above can not inappropriately be referred to the understanding and the inclination, so that in [the heart's] two most important parts, as said above, we may strive to lift up our hearts to God with the hands[65] of virtuous endeavor and spiritual exercise. All of us, if I am not mistaken, are seeking the things that are above with the understanding of faith and the judgment of reason, but perhaps we do not all equally savor the things above, enticed as we are to those which are on earth by some impetuous predisposition of the affections.

57. Tt 2:14
58. Heb 4:12
59. Ps 87:4 (88:3); Si 51:9
60. Pr 31:19
61. 2 Co 1:7
62. Rv 3:16
63. Jb 3:5, 10:22, etc.
64. Col 3:1-2
65. Lm 3:41

What is the source of that great diversity of characters we pointed out a little earlier, that dissimilarity in enthusiasms, that difference in ways of life? Why is the spiritual gift[66] so absent from
some while there is such abundance for others? Certainly, the
Dispenser of grace is neither miserly nor indigent, but where there
are no empty vessels, the oil must stop flowing.[67] On all sides
the love of the world pours itself in; with its consolations, or rather
desolations, it watches at the door, rushes in through the windows,[68] and seizes the mind—but not [the mind] of the one who
said: 'My soul refused to be consoled; I was mindful of God and
found delight.'[69] Holy delight assuredly turns away from the
mind preoccupied with worldly desires,[70] for the true cannot be
mixed with the false, nor the eternal with the transitory, nor the
spiritual with the physical, nor the highest with the lowest. Consequently, you cannot equally savor the things above and the
things on earth.

9. Fortunate [were] those men, through whom, we read, the
Lord's ascension was prefigured, Enoch [who was] caught up[71]
and Elijah [who was] taken up.[72] Clearly fortunate are they who
now live solely for God,[73] [and] are free to do nothing more than
understand, love and enjoy [God]. In those who are known to
have walked with God,[74] the perishable bodies do not press down
the souls, and the earthly dwelling does not burden the mind
that ponders many things.[75] Every obstacle has been taken from
[their] midst, every occasion removed; no material has been left
to press down their inclination or burden their understanding.
Scripture recalls that [Enoch] was caught up so that wickedness
would not conquer wisdom,[76] and that his understanding or soul
would be deceived or altered no more.[77]

10. But for us in this darkness what [will be] the source of truth?
What [will be] the source of charity in this wicked world,[78] in this
world which has been put in the power of the evil one?[79] Do you
think there will be anyone to enlighten our understanding, to
enkindle our inclination? Of course there will be, if we turn to
Christ, so that the veil may be removed from [our] hearts.[80] He
is the one of whom it is written: 'On those dwelling in the land

66. Rm 1:11	67. 2 K 4:3-6	68. Jr 9:20-21
69. Ps 76:3-4 (77:2-3)	70. Tt 2:12	71. Gn 5:22; Si 44:16
72. 2 K 2:11, Si 48:9	73. 2 Co 5:15	74. Gn 5:22
75. Ws 9:15	76. Ws 7:30	77. Ws 4:11
78. Ga 1:4	79. 1 Jn 5:19	80. 2 Co 3:15-16

of the shadow of death, on them has light risen.'[81] According to what Paul related to the Athenians, God overlooked times of earlier ignorance, but now calls on people everywhere to repent.[82] Keep in mind the Word of God[83] and Wisdom incarnate:[84] during the whole time that that unutterable strength, that glory, that majesty deigned to be seen on earth and to live among humans,[85] his work was surely to enlighten the eyes of the heart[86] and to persuade people to believe both by his preaching and the signs he displayed. Moreover 'The Spirit of the Lord is upon me;' he says; 'he has sent me to preach the good news to the poor.'[87] And to the apostles he would say: 'The light is among you only a little while longer; walk while you have the light, so that darkness will not overtake you.'[88] Not just before [his] passion, but even after [his] resurrection, when 'in many convincing ways he appeared to them during the forty days and spoke about the kingdom of God,'[89] and, as we read, he opened their minds to understand the Scriptures,[90] he was informing [their] understanding more than purifying [their] inclination.

11. Now how could the sense-bound be directed toward what is spiritual? Nay, they could not endure the plain light itself even for a little while! The Word had to be shown them in the flesh, the sun in a cloud, the light in an earthen jug, the honey in wax, the candle in a lantern. A Spirit before their face [was] Christ the Lord, but [he was] not without a shadow under which they could live for now among the nations.[91] So we read that the [Spirit] cast a shadow over the Virgin too,[92] lest, beaten back by too dazzling a splendor, even the keen sight of that eagle be weakened before the most brilliant light and perfectly pure brightness of the divinity.

Yet that gentle cloud[93] could not be useless; it, too, worked to bring about [our] salvation. [Christ] aroused the disciples' inclination toward his own flesh because, without some modification of will, their minds could not be directed toward understanding of faith, and [they] did not yet have the strength to rise up toward what is spiritual. Thus they would cling to [this] man [who was] performing wondrous deeds and uttering wondrous words

81. Is 9:2   82. Ac 17:30   83. Heb 6:5
84. 1 Co 1:24   85. Ba 3:38   86. Eph 1:18
87. Lk 4:18   88. Jn 12:35   89. Ac 1:3
90. Lk 24: 32   91. Lm 4:20   92. Lk 1:35
93. Is 19:1

with a human sort of love. Assuredly [their] love was still carnal, but so strong as to prevail over all other loves. This was surely the serpent of Moses that devoured all the serpents of the Egyptian magicians.[94] Moreover, 'Behold,' they say, 'we have left everything and followed you.'[95]

Truly blessed are the eyes that saw[96] the Lord of majesty present in the flesh, the Source of the universe when he lived among humankind,[97] radiant with virtues, curing the sick, treading on the seas, raising up the dead,[98] commanding demons, [and] conferring on human beings a like power.[99] [They saw him] meek and humble in heart,[100] kind, approachable, [and] overflowing with tender compassion,[101] the Lamb of God,[102] having no sin but bearing the sins of all. Blessed are the ears[103] found worthy to gather the words of life[104] from the very mouth of the Word incarnate; to them 'the Only-begotten who is at the Father's side' explained[105] and made known whatever he heard from the Father.[106] Thus they might drink in the perfectly pure source of truth itself, the streams of heavenly teaching; they were to absorb what was later to be poured out, or even spouted forth, to all peoples.

12. Should we wonder, brothers, that sorrow filled their heart[s][107] when he announced that he was about to leave them and added: 'Where I am going, you cannot come now'?[108] Why would their inner selves not be shaken up, their emotions not be troubled, their mind[s] not quaver, their countenances not be dismayed, [and] their hearing not be appalled? How could the message of his departure be received with complete calmness, when he for whom they had left everything was going to leave them?[109] Yet he had not focused all the disciples' affection onto his flesh so that it would remain with his flesh,[110] but so that it might be transferred to the Spirit. Thus the time would come when they would say: 'Even though we knew Christ according to the flesh, now we no longer know him [that way].'[111] Therefore that kindest of Masters, comforting them with gentle consolations, says: 'I will ask my Father and he will give you another

94. Ex 7:12	95. Mt 19:27	96. Lk 10:23; Mt 13:16
97. Ba 3:38	98. Mt 10:8; 14:25	99. Mt 9:8
100. Mt 11:29	101. Lk 1:78	102. Jn 1:29
103. Mt 13:16	104. Jn 6:69	105. Jn 1:18
106. Jn 15:15	107. Jn 16:6	108. Jn 8:21; Jn 13:33
109. Mt 19:27	110. Ph 1:24	111. 2 Co 5:16

Paraclete, the Spirit of truth[112] who will remain with you forever.' Again he says: 'I tell you the truth: it is for your good that I go. For unless I go, the Paraclete will not come.'[113]

[There is] a great mystery, my brothers. What does this mean: 'Unless I go, the Paraclete will not come'? Was the presence of Christ repugnant to the Paraclete? Did the Holy Spirit shudder at cohabiting with the Lord's flesh, which, as we know from the Angel's message, could not have been conceived without the Spirit's coming upon [Mary]?[114] What does this mean then: 'Unless I go, the Paraclete will not come'? [He means that] unless the presence of the flesh is withdrawn from your sight, your busy mind does not admit the fullness of spiritual grace; [your] mind does not receive it nor [your] inclination embrace it.

13. How does it seem to you,[115] brothers? If these things are so, or rather because they are so, would anyone who in other respects gives in to some alluring fantasies, who follows the enticements of his flesh—the flesh is indeed a sinful woman, begotten in sin, accustomed to sin, and in whom there is no good—[would such a one] dare to wait for the Paraclete? I say, who cleaves continually to this dung-heap, who cherishes the flesh,[116] sows in the flesh,[117] [and] savors the flesh,[118] would he dare [to expect] the consolation of nothing less than a celestial visitation, the torrent of delight,[119] the grace of the mighty Spirit?[120] As the Truth himself bears witness,[121] the apostles could in no way receive [the Spirit] while [they were] with the flesh of the Word. Anyone is completely mistaken to think that heavenly sweetness could be mixed with these ashes, divine balm with this poison, or the gifts of the Spirit with enticements of this type.

You are mistaken, holy Thomas, you are mistaken if you hope to see the Lord when [you are] apart from the company of the apostles.[122] Truth has no love for corners; roadside lodging places[123] do not please him. Truth stands in the open[124] and delights in discipline, the common life, and common undertakings. Wretch, how long will you go looking for side roads, seeking the consolations of self-will with such great effort, and begging

---

112. Jn 14:16-17
113. Jn 16:7
114. Lk 1:35
115. Mt 18:12
116. Eph 5:29
117. Ga 6:8
118. Rm 8:5
119. Ps 35:9 (36:8)
120. Ac 2:2
121. Jn 16:7
122. Jn 20:24-25
123. Lk 2:7
124. Jn 20:26

for [them] so disgracefully? 'And what am I to do?' you ask. 'Cast out the maid-servant and her son; for the son of the maid-servant shall not be an heir with the son of a free woman.'[125] As I have said, [there is] no accord between truth and vanity, light and darkness, spirit and flesh, fire and lukewarmness.[126]

14. 'But while the [Spirit] delays,' you will say, 'I cannot be without some consolation.' On the contrary, 'if he seems slow, wait for him, because he will come and will not delay.'[127] The apostles sat waiting ten days, 'continuing together in prayer with the women and Mary, the mother of Jesus.'[128] You too, then, learn to pray, learn to seek, to ask, to knock until you find, until you receive, until it is opened to you.[129] The Lord knows your creation:[130] he is faithful, he does not allow you to be tried beyond your ability.[131] I trust in him; if you wait faithfully he will not even wait for the tenth day. Surely he will come to meet the desolate but praying soul with his choicest blessings.[132] And so, refusing to be consoled,[133] happily and not foolishly,[134] you find delight in thinking of him,[135] being filled with his abundant stores, and quenched with the torrent of his delight.[136]

This is undoubtedly the way that Elisha once prayed when, as we read, he lamented that his sweet solace, Elijah's presence, was to be taken from him.[137] Yet consider carefully how he prayed, and what response was given to him as he pleaded. 'I pray, Lord,' he says, 'that your spirit may be twofold in me.'[138] It was appropriate that the spirit be twofold in him, so that a twofold measure of grace would compensate for the absence of [his] departing master. For this reason Elijah said to him: 'If you see [me] when I am being taken from you, what you ask shall be.'[139] The sight of him leaving made twofold his spirit, when, visibly caught up to heaven,[140] he bore with him every desire of Elisha, so that he too would then begin to savor the things that are above, not those on the earth.[141] The sight of [Elijah] leaving made twofold his spirit, so that to spiritual understanding[142] was joined spiritual inclina-

---

125. Ga 4:30   126. 2 Co 6:14-16
127. Hab 2:3, as in the antiphon *Ecce apparebit*, for the Second Sunday
     of Advent. Cf. Ascension 5.1, n. 7.
128. Ac 1:14   129. Mt 7:7-8   130. Ps 102:14 (103:14)
131. 1 Co 10:13   132. Ps 20:4 (21:3) 133. Ps 76:3 (77:2)
134. Ps 21:3 (22:2) 135. Ps 76:4 (77:3) 136. Ps 35:9 (36:8)
137. 2 K 2:9   138. 2 K 2:9   139. 2 K 2:10
140. 2 Co 12:2   141. Col 3:2   142. Col 1:9

tion, which was caught up to heaven with the very flesh to which it was so strongly clinging.

15. We find this quite obviously fulfilled in the apostles. When that Jesus of theirs was so manifestly lifted up,[143] and was being taken into heaven as they looked on,[144] so that none of them needed to ask: 'Where are you going?'[145] then, by faith that has been given eyes, so to speak, they were taught to raise their eyes beseechingly up to heaven,[146] [and] to stretch out pure hands[147] as they besought the gifts of charismatic grace promised them. [They did this] until suddenly from heaven was heard the sound of the mighty Spirit coming,[148] of the fire coming that the Lord Jesus was sending to earth,[149] desiring that it be mightily enkindled.

Certainly they had also received the Spirit earlier, that is, when he breathed on them and said: 'Receive the Holy Spirit.'[150] But there was need for the spirit to be twofold, plainly the spirit of faith and understanding, not of fervor, [the spirit] that would enlighten their reason more than it would inflame their inclination. For first the Word of the Father had taught them discipline and wisdom, and filled their hearts with understanding;[151] afterwards the divine Fire, coming upon them and finding them clean vessels, abundantly poured out gifts of charismatic grace and completely transformed their love into spiritual love. A charity strong as death blazed up in them[152] [and] scorned closing, for fear of the Jews,[153] not just [their] doors but even [their] mouths.

In preparation for that grace, let us strive, dearly beloved, in the measure our littleness [allows], to empty ourselves of all things[154] and to rid our hearts of wretched pleasures and transitory consolations. Now with the feast day pressing upon us, let us persevere with one accord in prayer,[155] with greater fervor and increased faithfulness, that the kind Spirit, the sweet Spirit, the strong Spirit, may deign [to bestow] on us his visitation, his consolation and strengthening: strengthening what is weak, smoothing what is rough, and purifying [our] hearts, that [Spirit] who is one with the Father and Son, the same but not identical. For that three are one and one is three is professed in perfect truth

143. Ac 1:9 144. Lk 24:51 145. Jn 16:5
146. Lk 18:13 147. 1 Tm 2:8 148. Ac 2:2
149. Lk 12:49 150. Jn 20:22 151. Pr 1:2; Si 15:5; 17:5-6
152. Sg 8:6 153. Jn 20:19 154. Ph 2:7
155. Ac 1:14

and faithfulness by the universal Church, [which has been] adopted by the Father, espoused by the Son, [and] strengthened by
the Spirit: to whom as there is one substance, so is there no less
one glory forever and ever.[156] Amen.

156. Rm 16:27

pentecost

Sermon One
THE HOLY SPIRIT, HOW HE WORKS IN US THREE WAYS

We celebrate today, dearly beloved, the solemn feast of the Holy Spirit, one to be celebrated with complete joyfulness, deserving our full devotion. The Holy Spirit is something of perfect sweetness in God, the kindness of God,[1] and is himself very God. Accordingly, if we celebrate the saints' solemn feasts, how much more should we celebrate his, from whom all who were saints derived their saintliness? If we venerate the sanctified, how much more appropriate is it that the Sanctifier himself be honored?

Today, then, is the Holy Spirit's festival, on which he, the invisible, appeared visibly; just as the Son, although he was no less invisible in himself, deigned to display himself visibly in the flesh. Today the Holy Spirit reveals to us something about himself, just as earlier we learned something about the Father and the Son. Perfect knowledge of the Trinity is life eternal.[2] Yet now we know only in part;[3] the remainder, which we can but little comprehend, we take on faith. Concerning the Father, I know creation. Created beings cry out: 'He made us, and not we ourselves.'[4] 'For since the creation of the world the invisible [nature] of God has been clearly perceived, understood through the things that have been made.'[5] But his eternity and immutability are too much for me to comprehend: 'He dwells in light inaccessible.'[6] Concerning the Son, I know something great by his gift, namely, his incarnation. 'For who shall declare his descent?'[7] Who can comprehend one begotten as the equal of his begettor? Concerning the Holy Spirit, [I] now [know something] too, if not the procession by which he proceeds from the Father and the Son—that 'knowledge has become wonderful to me; it is high and I cannot attain to it'[8]— still, I know something, namely his breathing. This has two aspects: whence it proceeds, and whither [it goes].[9] The procession from the Father and the Son 'has made darkness its hiding

1. Rm 2:4
2. Jn 17:3
3. 1 Co 13:9
4. Ps 99:3 (100:3)
5. Rm 1:20
6. 1 Tm 6:16
7. Is 53:8
8. Ps 138:6 (139:6)
9. Jn 3:8

place';[10] but today the procession toward human beings began to become known, and has now been manifested to the faithful.

2. At the beginning, indeed, since it was necessary, the invisible Spirit declared his advent by visible signs. At the present time, in that they are more spiritual, his signs seem more appropriate, more worthy of the Holy Spirit. Then the Spirit came upon the disciples in tongues of fire,[11] that they might speak words of fire and preach the law of fire[12] of the tongue of fire. Let no one complain that that manifestation of the Spirit is not made to us, for 'the manifestation of the Spirit is given to each one for a good purpose.'[13] Then, if it must be said, that manifestation was made for us rather than for the apostles. For what purpose were the tongues of the nations necessary to them, if not for the conversion of the nations?

Among them was yet another manifestation, pertaining more to them; and this one is made to us even until today. For it was manifested that they were clothed with 'power from on high':[14] from great timidity of spirit[15] they attained great steadfastness! This is not the time for fleeing, for hiding from fear of the Jews![16] Now they are more constant in their preaching than they had previously been fearful in their skulking. Furthermore, the earlier fright of the prince of the apostles at the words of a maidservant[17] [and] his later fortitude under the lashings of the chief men manifestly demonstrate this change [made by] the right hand of the Most High.[18] 'They went out from the presence of the council,' says Scripture, 'rejoicing that they were accounted worthy to suffer reproach for the name of Jesus.'[19] Earlier, when [Jesus] was being led to the council, they had fled and left him alone.[20] Who can doubt that a mighty Spirit[21] had come, who would enlighten their minds with an invisible power? In this way, even now, those things worked by the Spirit within us[22] bear witness to him.

3. Therefore, since we have received a commandment[23] that, turning away from evil, we should do what is good,[24] see how in both of these things the Spirit assists our weakness.[25] 'There

---

10. Ps 17:12 (18:11)   11. Ac 2:3   12. Dt 33:2
13. 1 Co 12:7   14. Lk 24:49   15. Ps 54:9 (55:8)
16. Jn 20:19   17. Mt 26:69-72   18. Ps 76:11 (77:10)
19. Ac 5:41   20. Mt 26:56   21. Ac 2:2
22. 1 Co 12:11; Ga 3:5   23. 2 Jn 4
24. Ps 36:27 (37:27); 2 Co 13:7   25. Rm 8:26

are varieties of gifts, but the same Spirit.'[26] And so, for turning away [from evil] the Spirit brings about three things in us: compunction, petition, and forgiveness. The first step in returning to God is repentance, which surely the Spirit, not ours but God's, brings about. This unerring reason teaches and authority too confirms. Will anyone who comes shivering to a fire and is warmed [by it] question that the heat, which he could not have had without the fire, came to him from it? In the same way, if someone once freezing because of his iniquity is afterwards inflamed by a certain fervor of repentance, should he question whether it was another Spirit that had come to him, one who accuses and judges his own? You find this in the gospel when, speaking of the Spirit whom those who believed in him were to receive,[27] [Jesus] said, 'He will accuse the world of sin.'[28]

4. But of what benefit is it to repent of a fault and not to petition for forgiveness? It is necessary that the Spirit bring this about too, filling the mind with a certain sweet hope, through which you may ask in faith, with no doubting.[29] Do you want me to show you that this, too, is the work of the Holy Spirit? Surely while he is absent you will find nothing of this kind in your own spirit. Moreover, he is the one 'in whom we cry, Abba, Father,'[30] he is the one who asks with unspeakable groanings on behalf of the saints.[31] And these things [he brings about] in our hearts. What then does he do in the Father's [heart]? Just as within us he intercedes for us,[32] so within the Father he forgives our trespasses, with the Father himself.[33] In our hearts, he is our Advocate before the Father;[34] in the Father's heart, he is our Lord. Thus it is the [Spirit] himself; who grants what we ask, who grants that we may ask. Just as he lifts us up by a certain loving trust, so with a mercy even more loving he inclines God toward us. That you may be entirely certain that the Spirit brings about the forgiveness of sins, listen to what the apostles once heard: 'Receive the Holy Spirit. If you forgive the sins of any, they are forgiven them.'[35] This is how he works in turning us away from evil.

5. But what does the good Spirit bring about in us that we may do good? In fact he admonishes, he moves, and he instructs. He

26. 1 Co 12:4   27. Jn 7:39   28. Jn 16:8
29. Jm 1:6   30. Rm 8:15   31. Rm 8:26-27
32. Rm 8: 34   33. Col 2:13   34. 1 Jn 2:1
35. Jn 20:22-23

admonishes our memory; he instructs our reason; he moves our
will. Our whole soul consists of these three [faculties]. To the
memory he suggests good things in holy thoughts, and in this
way he drives away our listlessness and sloth. Therefore as often as you perceive a suggestion of this type of good in your heart,
give glory to God,[36] and show reverence to the Holy Spirit, whose
voice is sounding in your ears.[37] Truly it is he who speaks justice.[38] In the gospel you find that 'he will suggest to you all that
I have said to you.'[39] And notice what precedes: 'He will teach
you all things.'

I have said that he instructs our reason. Many indeed are admonished to do good, but have little idea of what to do unless
the grace of the Spirit is present [to us] anew. May he teach us
to carry out in deed the thought which he inspires, lest God's
grace in us be fruitless![40] But what more [does he do]? 'For anyone to know the good and not to do it is, for him, a sin.'[41] For
that reason we need not only to be admonished and taught, but
to be moved as well, and influenced toward good by the same
Spirit who assists our weakness,[42] and through whom the charity that is a good will is spread abroad in our hearts.[43]

6. When the Spirit comes this way he possesses the entire soul
by suggesting, by instructing, and by influencing. He is always
speaking in our thoughts, so that we too may hear what the Lord
God speaks within us.[44] He enlightens our reason and enkindles
our will. Does it not seem to you that cloven tongues, as of fire,
are filling the whole house [of the soul][45]? For it has been said
above that the whole soul consists of these three [faculties]. Moreover, the tongues may be cloven because of our many thoughts,
but their multiplicity may be like fire in [being] one light, of truth,
and one heat, of charity. Or the filling of the house may be reserved for the end, when there will be put into our laps good
measure, pressed down and shaken together and running over.[46]

But when will these things take place? Surely, when the days
of Pentecost have been fulfilled.[47] Fortunate are you who have
already entered into the fiftieth [day] of repose and the jubilee

36. Jn 9:24; Ac 12:23   37. Sg 2:14   38. Is 45:19
39. Jn 14:26   40. 1 Co 15:10   41. Jm 4:17
42. Rm 8:26   43. Rm 5:5   44. Ps 84:9 (85:8)
45. Ac 2:2-3   46. Lk 6:38   47. Ac 2:1

year![48] I am speaking of our brothers to whom the Spirit has already said 'that they may rest from their labors.'[49] For this too we find among his works. Indeed we celebrate two seasons, brothers: one of forty days, the other of fifty days; one before the passion, the other after the resurrection; one in compunction of heart and wails of repentence, the other in dedication of spirit and the alleluia of the festival. The first season is that of [our] present life; the second signifies the repose of the saints that comes after death. But when the end of the fifty days has come, in the judgment and resurrection, with the days of Pentecost fulfilled, the fullness of the Spirit will be present and will fill the entire house. Full indeed will be the whole earth with his majesty,[50] when not only our soul, but even our spiritual body, will rise, if, in accordance with the Apostle's admonition, it has been sown while still a physical body.[51]

48. Lv 25:10-11   49. Rv 14:13   50. Is 6:3; Ps 71:19 (72:19)
51. 1 Co 15:44

[pentecost]

Sermon Two
THE WORKS OF THE TRINITY UPON US,
THE CONCERN OF THE SON,
AND THE THREEFOLD GRACE OF THE HOLY SPIRIT

TODAY, DEARLY BELOVED, 'the heavens distilled rain from the presence of the God of Sinai, from the presence of the God of Israel, and a freely given rain was reserved' for Christ's inheritance.[1] The Holy Spirit, proceeding from the Father,[2] came upon the apostles with the generous largesse of his majesty, and bestowed upon them gifts of charismatic grace. Indeed, after the eminence of his resurrection, after the glory of his ascension, after the sublimity of his enthronement, what remained but that the joy [which was] the expectation of the just[3] should come, and that those destined for glory should be filled with heavenly gifts.

But see whether Isaiah, by the weight of his thoughts and the order of his words, did not foretell all these things long before. 'In that day,' he says, 'the branch of the Lord shall be in magnificence and glory, and the fruit of the earth [shall be] sublime, and great joy [shall come] to those of Israel who have been saved.'[4] The 'branch of the Lord' is Christ Jesus, alone conceived of perfectly clean seed.[5] Although in the likeness of sinful flesh,[6] nevertheless he was not in sinful flesh; although a child of Adam's flesh, nevertheless he was not a child of Adam's transgression.[7] He was not by nature a child of wrath,[8] like all the rest, who were conceived in iniquities.[9] Therefore this branch that sprouted from Jesse's rod with virginal greenness was 'in magnificence' when he rose up from the dead, since then, 'O Lord my God, you were exceedingly great,' arrayed in praise and beauty, 'clothed with light as with a garment.'[10] How great the 'glory' of your ascension, when, in the midst of angels and saintly souls, you are led to the Father, and, brought into the heavens with the triumphal palm, you enclose the humanity [you] took on in the very identity of divinity? Who can ponder, much less utter, how 'sublime'

---

1. Ps 67:9-10 (68:8-9)   2. Jn 15:26   3. Pr 10:28
4. Is 4:2   5. Jb 14:4   6. Rm 8:3
7. Rm 5:14   8. Eph 2:3   9. Ps 50:7 (51:5)
10. Ps 103:1-2 (104:1-2)

is 'the fruit of the earth' when seated at the right hand of the Father, how he dazzles even the eyes of heavenly natures, how angelic insight quakes [and] does not grasp it? Therefore, let 'the great joy' come, Lord Jesus, 'to those of Israel who have been saved,' to your apostles, whom you chose before the foundation of the world.[11] Let your good Spirit[12] come to wash away impurities and infuse virtues 'in a spirit of judgment and a spirit of burning.'[13]

2. Come then, brothers, let us consider ourselves, and the actions of the Trinity in us, from the beginning of the world until the end. Let us see how that Majesty upon whom lie both the administration and the governance of the ages has been concerned not to lose us forever. Indeed he had made all things mightily, and he was governing all things wisely. Perfectly apparent signs of both realities, his power and his wisdom, were contained in the creation and the conservation of this worldly machine. There was goodness in God, goodness great beyond measure; but it lay concealed in the heart of the Father, to be lavished at a seasonable time[14] upon the race of the children of Adam.

Yet the Lord was saying, 'I think thoughts of peace,'[15] that he might send us the One who is our peace, 'who made both one';[16] that he might now bestow peace upon peace, peace to those far away and peace to those who are near.[17] His own kindness, then, induced the Word of God, who was on high, to come down to us; his compassion drew him; the truth by which he had promised that he would come compelled him; the purity of a virginal womb received him, while the virgin's integrity remained intact; virtue reared him; obedience steered him in all things; patience armed him; [and] charity revealed him by words and miracles.

3. Certainly, I now have very ample material, both about my evils and about the good things of my Lord, so that when I have pondered my ways I may turn my feet to his testimonies.[18] Those good things are inexpressible, because, to sum it all up briefly, the Wisdom of God in his utter wisdom could find no better way to redeem us. But evils also surrounded us, [evils] without num-

---

11. Eph 1:4   12. Lk 11:13   13. Is 4:4
14. Ps 31:6 (32:6)
15. Jr 29:11; see Introit *Dixit Dominus* formerly used on the Second Sunday after Pentecost.
16. Eph 2:14   17. Eph 2:17   18. Ps 118:59 (119:59)

ber.[19] 'My sins,' as a just man says, 'outnumber the sands of the seashore,'[20] and, 'For your name's sake, O Lord, may you pardon my sin, for it is great.'[21] A sinuous serpent[22] was sent by the devil to pour poison through the woman's ears into her mind, and thus to pour it out in the source of all future generations. However, the angel Gabriel was sent from God[23] to utter the Word of the Father through the Virgin's ear into her womb and mind, [and] to enable the antidote to enter by the same way by which the poison had entered. Truly 'we have seen his glory, glory as of the only-begotten of the Father.'[24] What Christ has brought us from the Father's heart is wholly fatherly, in order that humankind's anxiety might surmise that there is in the Son of God nothing that is not good and fatherly. From the sole of our foot to the top of our head there was no health in us.[25] We had gone astray from the womb,[26] condemned in the womb before we were born, because we were conceived from sin and in sin.[27]

4. Christ, then, first applied the balm to the place first wounded. Having in his essence entered the Virgin's womb, he was conceived of the Holy Spirit to purify our conception, which an evil spirit had, if not effected, then infected. Thus [Christ's] life even in the womb would not be useless: during those nine months he cleanses the ancient wound, probing, as it is said, the foul festering sore even to its depths in order to ensure everlasting health. Even then he was bringing about our 'salvation in the midst of the earth,'[28] in the womb of the Virgin Mary, called 'the midst of the earth' with wonderful precision, for to her—as to the midst [of the earth], as to the ark of God, as to the cause of [all] things, as to the managing of the ages—all who dwell in heaven, as well as those who dwell in hell, look for help; those who have gone before us, we who [now] are, those who will follow us, their children's children, and their offspring after them. Those in heaven look to her to be restored; those in hell to be delivered. Those who have gone before us [look to her] that the prophets may be found worthy of belief;[29] those who follow us that they may win glory.

19. Ps 39:13 (40:12)
20. Responsory *Peccavi* used for the Fourth Sunday after Pentecost.
21. Ps 24:11 (25:11)   22. Gn 3:1-6; Jb 26:13   23. Lk 1:26-38
24. Jn 1:14   25. Is 1:6   26. Ps 57:4 (58:3)
27. Ps 50:7 (51:5)   28. Ps 73:12 (74:12)   29. Si 36:15-18

On that account 'all generations call you blessed,'[30] O Begetter of God, Sovereign Lady of the world, Queen of heaven. 'All generations,' I repeat, for there are generations of heaven and of earth.[31] 'Father of spirits,'[32] the Apostle says, 'from whom all fatherhood in heaven and on earth takes its name.'[33] Henceforth, then, will all generations call you blessed, you who brought forth life and glory for all generations. In you the angels find gladness, the righteous grace, [and] sinners forgiveness forever. Rightly do the eyes of all creatures look to you,[34] because in you, and through you, and from you the gracious hand of the Almighty recreated whatever he had created.

5. Will it please you, Lord Jesus, to give your life for me as you have given [your] conception? Because not only is my conception impure, but my death [is] not right, my life full of risks, and after death there waits a more grievous death, the second death.[35] 'Not only my conception,' [Jesus] says, 'but my life too—and this during every one of life's stages, infancy, boyhood, adolescence, and young manhood— will I give for you; adding to it death and resurrection, ascension and the sending of the Holy Spirit. This [I will do] in order that my conception may cleanse yours, my life instruct yours, my death destroy yours, my resurrection herald yours, my ascension prepare for yours, and finally, that the Spirit may assist you in your weakness.[36] Thus will you see clearly the way by which you should walk,[37] and the care with which you should walk, and the destination to which you should walk. In my life you will recognize your way; and as I held to the unswerving paths of poverty and obedience, humility and patience, charity and mercy, so you too must also walk in [my] footsteps, turning aside neither to right nor to left.[38] In my death, I will give you my righteousness, shattering the yoke of your captivity, subduing the enemies who are on your way or alongside your way, that they may not draw near to harm you further.[39] When those things have been done, 'I will return to my house from which I come';[40] and I will turn my face toward those sheep that remained on the mountains.[41] I left them for your sake, not that I might lead you, but that I might carry you back.

---

30. Lk 1:48
31. Gn 2:4
32. Heb 12:9
33. Eph 3:15
34. 1 K 1:20
35. Rv 20:14
36. Rm 8:26
37. Ps 142:8 (143:8)
38. Nb 20:17
39. Ps 88:23 (89:22)
40. Lk 11:24
41. Mt 18:12

6. 'And lest you complain or sorrow at my absence, I will send you the Spirit, the Paraclete,[42] who will give you the pledge of salvation, the force of life, and the light of knowledge. [He will give you] the pledge of salvation, that the Spirit himself may bear witness that you are a child of God.[43] He will show you, and impress on your heart, unmistakeable signs of your predestination.[44] He will put gladness in your heart,[45] and with the dew of heaven[46] will he satisfy your mind, if not constantly, then very often. [He will give you] the force of life, that what is by nature impossible for you will through his grace be made not only possible but even easy. Thus you will proceed with delight, as 'in all riches,'[47] in labors, in vigils, in hunger and thirst,[48] and in all the observances which, unless sweetened with this meal, may seem [to be] 'death in the pot.'[49] [He will give you] the light of knowledge, so that when you have done all things well you may consider yourself an unprofitable servant;[50] and whatever good you find in yourself, you may attribute to him from whom comes all good and without whom you cannot begin, much less complete, even the smallest task.

So, therefore, in these three things will the Spirit himself teach you all things,[51] all things concerning your salvation, because in these three is complete and absolute perfection.'

7. This is how the same Spirit speaks through the prophet: 'Sow for yourselves righteousness,'[52] where the pledge of salvation is revealed. Reap the hope of life, where the vital force is received. Light for yourselves the lamp of knowledge, which needs no explanation. Hence this Spirit appeared on the apostles in [the form of] fire,[53] because of its light and equally of its heat. For he causes those whom he has filled to be fervent in spirit, and to recognize in truth that it is mercy alone which both anticipates and guides them. [David,] the Lord's servant, drew many threads together from all sides on the subject of mercy when he said: 'His mercy will go before me';[54] and, 'Your mercy is before my eyes';[55] and, 'Your mercy will follow me all the days of my life';[56] and, 'He crowns me with mercy and compassion';[57] and

42. Jn 15:26   43. Rm 8:16
44. Cf. Bernard's Sermon One for Septuagesima, 1.1; SBOp, 4: 345.
45. Ps 4:7   46. Gn 27:28   47. Ps 118:14 (119:14)
48. 2 Co 6:5, 11:27   49. 2 K 4:40-41   50. Lk 17:10
51. Jn 14: 26   52. Ho 10:12   53. Ac 2:3
54. Ps 58:11 (59:10)   55. Ps 25:3 (26:3)   56. Ps 22:6 (23:6)
57. Ps 102:4 (103:4)

'My God, my mercy!'[58] How delightfully, Lord Jesus, did you converse with humans![59] How abundantly did you lavish many and great goods on humans! How bravely you suffered equal amounts of humiliation and bitterness for humans, so we may suck honey from the rock and oil from the hardest stone,[60] from hard [stone] in the words, harder [stone] in the lashes, hardest [stone] in the horrors of the cross. Through all these he kept silent, as a lamb before its shearer, and did not open his mouth.[61] You see, therefore, how truly he spoke who said: 'The Lord takes thought for me.'[62] To redeem a servant the Father spares not his own Son;[63] the Son delivers himself up[64] most willingly; both send the Holy Spirit;[65] and 'the Spirit himself intercedes for us with unspeakable groanings.'[66]

8. O hard, and hardened, and hardhearted children of Adam, [who remain] unmoved by such great kindness, such blazing fire; so prodigious a flame of love, [and] so ardent a lover, who paid such an extravagant price for a worthless piece of goods. 'Not with perishable things like gold and silver' did [Jesus] redeem us, but with his own 'precious blood'[67] which he poured forth richly[68] as waves of blood flowed out[69] liberally from the five parts of Jesus' body. What more should he have done that he did not do?[70] He enlightened the blind,[71] brought back the stragglers, reconciled the guilty, justified the ungodly.[72] Thirty-three years he was seen on earth; he lived among humans;[73] he died for humans, he who spoke concerning the Cherubim and Seraphim and all the angelic powers and they came to be;[74] when he wills it, all power is there with him.[75]

What then does he who sought you with such concern [now] seek from you, if not that you walk concernedly with your God?[76] No one but the Holy Spirit causes this concern. It is he who probes the depth of our hearts,[77] he who discerns the thoughts and intentions of the heart.[78] He does not allow the slightest amount of chaff to settle inside the dwelling of a heart which he possesses, but consumes it in an instant with a fire of the most minute

---

58. Ps 58:18 (59:17)
59. Ba 3:38
60. Dt 32:13
61. Is 53:7; Ac 8:32
62. Ps 39:18 (40:17)
63. Rm 8:32
64. Eph 5:2
65. Jn 14:26; 15:26
66. Rm 8:26
67. 1 P 1:18-19
68. Tt 3:6
69. Si 50:3 (Vulg.)
70. Is 5:4
71. Ps 145:8 (146:8)
72. Rm 4:5
73. Ba 3:38
74. Ps 32:9 (33:9)
75. Ws 12:18
76. Mi 6:8
77. 1 Co 2:10
78. Heb 4:12

inspection. He is the sweet and gentle Spirit who bends our will, or rather straightens and directs it more fully toward his own so that we may be able to understand [his will] truly, love it fervently, and fulfill it effectually.

[pentecost]

Sermon Three
ALSO ON THE SAME SOLEMN FEAST

THE VERY SPIRIT whose solemn and special feast we celebrate today—I trust with special devotion—knows how joyfully I would share with you anything I shall have perceived
has been inspired in me by his heavenly goodness. It is he, in
fact, dearly beloved, who makes you sit not only in the city but
even in a single house,[1] that he may settle upon those seated,
and rest upon those who are humble and who tremble at his
words.[2] It is he who covered the Virgin with his shadow[3] to prepare the deity's entrance into her virginal body. He also strengthened the apostles, that he might clothe them with power from
on high,[4] that is, with the most burning love.

This is undoubtedly the breastplate the apostolic choir put on,
like a giant,[5] 'to wreak vengeance on the nations, to rebuke the
peoples, to bind their kings in shackles and their nobles in iron
fetters.'[6] Since they were being sent into the strong man's house
to tie him up and plunder his property,[7] there was need for very
great strength. How much was needed for them in other situa-
tions, that they might triumph over death—and lest the gates of
hell prevail against them,[8] were 'love strong as death' and 'zeal
unyielding as hell'[9] not thriving and triumphing within them!

They had been drinking in this zeal when they were considered intoxicated with wine.[10] In fact, [they were] intoxicated with
wine, but not with the [wine] the unbelievers thought intoxicated them. Surely, I say, [they were] intoxicated, but with a new
wine that the old wineskins[11] were not worthy to receive and were
not strong enough to contain.[12] For the true Vine[13] had poured
forth this wine from on high, a wine delighting the heart[14] while
not throwing the mind off balance, 'a wine bringing forth virgins,'[15] not [one that] causes even the wise to fall away.[16] [It is]
a new wine, but [it is] for those dwelling on earth. Once it was

1. Ac 2:2-3   2. Is 11:2-4; 66:2   3. Lk 1:35
4. Lk 24:49   5. 1 M 3:3   6. Ps 149:7-8
7. Mt 12:29   8. Mt 16:18   9. Sg 8:6
10. Ac 2:13   11. Mt 9:17   12. Jr 2: 13
13. Jn 15:1   14. Si 40:20; Ps 103:15 (104:15)   15. Zc 9:17
16. Si 19:2, as in RB 40:7

overflowing in great abundance in heaven, not in wineskins, nor in earthen pots,[17] but in 'the wine cellar,'[18] in spiritual storerooms. Wine was flowing through all the quarters and streets[19] of that city in which there is gladness of heart, not debauchery[20] of the flesh: for 'the earthborn and children of humanity'[21] did not have wine of its type.

2. Thus heaven was enjoying its own wine, [a wine of which] earth meanwhile was unaware. But not even earth was wholly in need; it was glorying in the flesh of Christ, for whose presence heaven was no less thirsting. Why then should there not have been a perfectly sure and entirely pleasing exchange[22] between heaven and earth, between angels and apostles, so that Christ's flesh would be offered to the former and heavenly wine to the latter, and the Spirit would be present on earth, the flesh in heaven, and thenceforward all things [would be] common[23] to all for eternity? 'Unless I go,' [Jesus] says, 'the Paraclete will not come to you.'[24] That is to say: If you do not give up what you love, you will not have what you desire. Therefore, 'it is for your good that I go';[25] you too are to pass from earth to heaven, from flesh to spirit. The Son is spirit, the Father is spirit, and the Holy Spirit is spirit. Indeed, the spirit before our face is Christ the Lord.[26] The Father, too, since he is spirit, seeks the kind of worshipers who will worship him in spirit and in truth.[27] Yet the Holy Spirit is, as it were, specially called 'spirit,' because he proceeds from both [the Father and the Son], being the perfectly firm and indissoluble bond of the Trinity; likewise [he is] just as appropriately [called] 'holy,' because he is the gift of the Father and the Son, making every creature holy: albeit the Father, too, is both spirit and holy, and the Son, in the same way, is both spirit and holy, 'from whom [are] all things, by whom [are] all things, and in whom [are] all things,' says the Apostle.[28]

3. We must ponder three things about the great work which this world is, namely what it is, how it exists, and for what purpose it was established. Inestimable power is shown, even in the existence of things, because they were created so many, so mar-

---

17. Lm 4:2   18. Sg 2:4   19. Sg 3:2
20. Eph 5:18   21. Ps 48:3 (Ps 49:2)
22. Cf. *O admirabile commercium,* antiphon at vespers for January 1.
23. Ac 2:44; 4:32   24. Jn 16:7   25. Jn 16:7
26. Lm 4:20 (an early version)   27. Jn 4:23-24   28. Rm 11:36

velous, so diversely and so generously. Clearly a unique wisdom is apparent in the manner [of creation], because some things were placed above, some below, and others most methodically in the middle. If you meditate on the purpose for which [the world] was made, there appears a kindness so beneficial and a benefit so kind that it could overwhelm even the most ungrateful by the multitude and magnitude of its gifts. Indeed all things were created out of nothing with perfect power; they were created beautiful with perfect wisdom, and useful with perfect kindness.

Nevertheless, we know that there were from the beginning, and we see that there still are among the children of humanity many who, weighed down by the full power of their senses in this perceptible world's inferior goods, give their entire selves to the things that were made, disregarding in what way and for what purpose they were made. What shall we call these people, if not carnal? I think they are very few now. We read, however, that at one time there were some whose greatest zeal and only concern was to investigate the measure and arrangement of created things, with the result that many not only neglected to examine the usefulness of things, but also high-mindedly scorned the things themselves, [and were] content with very meager and poor food. These men call themselves philosophers, but we rightly name them curious and vain.

4. Men more prudent than either of these [types] have followed them. Passing over the things that have been made and how they were made, they directed their mental acuteness to seeing the purpose for which things were made. It was not hidden from them that God made everything for his own purpose,[29] everything for those who belong to him;[30] yet differently for his own purpose and for his people. In these words, 'everything for his own purpose,' the source which comes first is indicated; but in these, 'everything for his people,' the resultant product is expressed instead. He made everything for his own purpose, that is, with gratuitous goodness; he made everything for his chosen,[31] that is, for their benefit. Goodness, then, is the efficient cause, and their benefit the final cause. These are spiritual men, who use this world as though they were not [using it],[32] and seek God in the simplicity of their heart[s],[33] not even pursuing the great

29. Pr 16:4 (Vulg.)   30. 2 Co 4:15   31. 2 Tm 2:10
32. 1 Co 7:31   33. Ws 1:1

matter of how this worldly machine is turned. The first [kind of]
men are filled with pleasure, the second with vanity, and the third
with truth.

5. I rejoice that you are of this school, that is, the Spirit's school,
where you can learn goodness, and discipline, and knowledge,[34]
and affirm with the holy one: 'I have understood more than all
my teachers.'[35] Why, I ask? Is it because I have clothed myself
in purple and fine linen,[36] and because I have had abundance
of sumptuous banquets? Is it because I have understood, or en-
deavored to understand, the wiles of Plato and the guiles of
Aristotle? Not at all, I say, but 'because I have sought your testimonies.'[37] Fortunate is the one who remains in this dwelling[38]
of the Holy Spirit so as to be able to understand the threefold
spirit about which the Lord's servant, understanding more than
his elders, used to sing: 'Do not cast me away from your face,
and do not take your holy spirit from me. Create a pure heart
in me, O God, and renew a right spirit within my flesh. Restore
the joy of your salvation to me, and strengthen me with a ruling
spirit.'[39] 'Holy Spirit': understand that he is designated by his
own name. [David] asks that he not be cast away from [the Lord's
face] like something impure, because this Spirit hates impurities,
and cannot dwell 'in a body subject to sin.'[40] It is characteristic
of him to banish sin, and also for him to hate sins; great purity
and great impurity will not remain together in a single dwelling.
Therefore, after the Holy Spirit, through 'the holiness without
which no one shall see God,'[41] has been received, does anyone
dare to appear before his face[42] as bathed and clean,[43] since who
can refrain from every evil, and who shall have restrained his actions, even if not his thoughts?

6. Yet because perverse and impure thoughts separate [us] from
God,[44] we must pray that [our] heart[s] be created pure in us,
because that certainly will be accomplished if a right spirit be renewed within our flesh.[45] Because [David] says 'right spirit,' it
can be connected, not inappropriately, with the Son. Stripping
us of our 'old nature,' he puts on us the new;[46] he has renewed

---

34. Ps 118:66 (119:66)   35. Ps 118:99 (119:99)   36. Lk 16:19
37. Ps 118:22 (119:22)   38. Dt 33:12
39. Ps 50:13, 12, 14 (51:11, 10, 12)
40. Ws 1:4   41. Heb 12:14   42. Ps 41:3 (42:2)
43. Jn 13:10   44. Ws 1:3   45. Ps 50:12 (51:10)
46. Col 3:9-10; Eph 4:22-24

us in the spirit of our mind as well as in our flesh, so that we may ponder what is right and walk in the newness of the Spirit, not in the oldness of the written word.[47] He brought a beautiful model of uprightness from heaven; from heaven he left it on earth, incorporating and instilling the sweetness of uprightness in all his works, just as [David] had foretold of him: 'The Lord is sweet and upright; for this reason he will give the law to transgressors on the way.'[48] Once the body has been set right through holy actions, and the heart purified, or rather renewed, by upright thoughts, saving joy is restored:[49] then you may walk in the light of God's countenance, and exult in his name all the day![50]

7. What is left then, but that you be strengthened with a 'ruling spirit'?[51] Understand that the ruling spirit is the Father: not because [he is] greater, but because [he] alone is from nothing, while from him is the Son, and from both the Holy Spirit. In what is this strengthening, if not in love? What other gift is as worthy of the Father? What other present is so fatherly? The Apostle asks: 'Who shall separate us from the love of Christ? Tribulation or distress, famine or nakedness, peril or the sword?'[52] You may be certain that neither death, nor life, nor the other things the Apostle lists so variously and boldly, will be able to separate us from the love of God which is in Christ Jesus.[53] Does not every part of this utterance indicate strengthening?

Do you know how to possess your property in holiness and honor, not in the passion of lust?[54] You have received a 'holy spirit.' Is it your will that whatever you want others to do to you, you also do to them,[55] and what you do not want done to you, you do not do to another?[56] You have received a 'right spirit' for service to your neighbor. This is the uprightness that each law commends, both that imparted to [our] nature and that handed down by Scripture. If now you persevere with strength in both aspects and in what pertains to each, you have received the 'ruling spirit' which alone God approves. Furthermore, the One who truly exists takes no delight in what exists at one moment and not at another, nor can eternity be pleased with such transitory

47. Rm 6:4; 7:6
50. Ps 88:16-17 (89:15-16)
53. Rm 8:38-39
56. Tb 4:16, quoted in RB 61:14

48. Ps 24:8 (25:8)
51. Ps 50:14 (51:12)
54. 1 Th 4:4-5

49. Ps 50:14 (51:12)
52. Rm 8:35
55. Mt 7:12

things. And so, if you want God to choose a part in you for himself, take care to exhibit the ruling spirit to him who is the true Ruler and Father of spirits,[57] just as you exhibit the holy spirit to yourself, and the right spirit to your neighbor.

8. Truly manifold is the Spirit who inspires the children of humanity in such manifold ways that there is no one who can hide from his heat.[58] He is bestowed on them for their benefit, for miracle-working, for salvation, for help, for consolation, and for fervor. For their benefit, he lavishly bestows the common goods of life on the good and the evil, on the worthy equally with the unworthy,[59] so that he may be seen to be unbounded in his [powers] of discernment. Ungrateful is the one who does not acknowledge the goodness of the Spirit in these things too! For miracle-working there are signs, portents, and the various virtues, produced by the agency of anyone, no matter who. He revives the ancient miracle, so that he may from those of the present build up our faith in those of the past. But because he bestows this grace on some without benefit to them, he is poured out in a third way, for salvation, when with our whole heart we return[60] to the Lord our God. Then [the Spirit] is given for help, when he aids our weakness[61] in every struggle. When he presents to our spirit the proof that we are children of God,[62] that inspiration is intended for [our] consolation. And [the Spirit] is given for fervor when, breathing powerfully in the hearts of the perfect, he enkindles a mighty flame of love, that they may glory not only in the hope of the children of God, but even in tribulations,[63] reckoning abuse as glory, disgrace as joy, and contempt as exaltation.

On all of us, if I am not mistaken, the Spirit has been bestowed for salvation, but not so for fervor. There are few who are filled with this spirit, few who strive to excel. Content with our difficulties, we do not endeavour to respire in that freedom, nor even to aspire toward it. Let us pray, brothers, that the days of Pentecost be fulfilled in us, the days of forgiveness, the days of exultation, the days of the truest jubilee,[64] and that by our bodily presence and equally our oneness of heart, the Holy Spirit may always find all of us in one place[65] because of our vowed stabil-

57. Heb 12:9   58. Ps 18:7 (19:6)   59. Mt 5:45
60. Jr 24:7   61. Rm 8:26   62. Rm 8:16
63. Rm 5:2-3 (Vulg.)   64. Lv 25:10   65. Ac 2:1

ity,[66] to the praise and glory[67] of the Church's bridegroom, Jesus Christ our Lord, who is over all, God forever blessed.[68]

66. RB 58:17   67. Ph 1:11   68. Rm 9:15

the BIRthday of saint John the Baptist

THE BURNING AND SHINING LAMP

BROTHERS, FAR FROM THOSE GATHERING here be the prophet's reproach, in which he condemns the meetings of the Jews, saying: 'Your assemblies are wicked.'[1] Surely these assemblies are not wicked; clearly [they are] holy, and religious, and full of grace, worthy of blessing. Indeed, you gather together for listening to God; you gather together for praising, for praying, for worshipping.[2] Each is a sacred gathering, pleasing to God and familiar to [his] angels. Stand then in reverence, brothers, stand with concern and a devout mind, especially in the place of prayer, and in this school of Christ and spiritual listening place.

Dearly beloved, do not consider the things that are seen and temporal, but rather those that are not seen, [that are] eternal.[3] Judge according to faith, not according to appearance.[4] We ought greatly to reverence each place,[5] and not believe that the number of men present is greater than that of angels. Indisputably the gate of heaven is standing open in both, the ladder is set up, [and] the angels are ascending and descending[6] upon the 'Son of man.'[7] This 'Son of man' is a giant:[8] heaven is his throne, earth his footstool.[9] His majesty is raised above the heaven,[10] yet he remains with us until the end of time.[11] The holy angels are ascending and descending to him, because Christ is one, the head and the body.[12]

2. And yet, not where the head is, but 'wherever the body is, there the eagles will gather,'[13] even though the head cannot be separated from the body. Moreover, he himself says: 'Where two or three are gathered together in my name, there am I in their midst.'[14] But perhaps someone will say: 'Where is Christ now? Show us Christ and that will satisfy us.'[15] Why are your eyes so inquisitive? Do you gather together for looking, and not rather for listening? 'The Lord God opened my ears,' says the proph-

---

1. Is 1:13 (Vulg.)   2. 1 Co 11:20-22   3. 2 Co 4:18
4. Jn 7:24; 2 Co 10:7   5. Gn 28:17   6. Gn 28:12
7. Jn 1:51   8. Ps 18:6 (19:5)   9. Is 66:1
10. Ps 8:2 (8:1)   11. Mt 28:20   12. Col 1:18; Mt 23:10
13. Mt 24:28   14. Mt 18:20   15. Jn 14:8

et.[16] He opened my ear, that I may hear what he says;[17] he has not given light to my eye,[18] that I may see his face. And certainly he has opened his ear to me; he has not unveiled [his] face. He stands behind the wall,[19] he hears and is heard, but not yet does he appear. He listens to those who pray; he teaches those who listen. 'Do you seek proof that it is Christ who speaks in me?'[20] 'It is I,' he says, 'who speak of justice.'[21] Why should he not speak with the mouth he himself fashioned? Why should the artificer not use his own tool as he pleases? Lord, open not only their ears, but also my lips,[22] for 'I will not restrain my lips, you know it, Lord.'[23] You do all things well; you make the deaf hear and the dumb speak.[24]

3. Listen, brothers, to what is said about John, the solemnity of whose birth is celebrated today. 'He was a burning and shining lamp,'[25] [Scripture] says. A great testimony, my brothers: great is the one to whom it is given, but greater is the one who gives [it]. 'He was a burning and shining lamp.' Only to shine is nothing; only to burn is not enough. To burn and shine is complete. Hear what Scripture says: 'The wise man endures like the sun, but the fool changes like the moon.'[26] The moon shines brightly without heat, now full, then waning, finally it seems no moon at all. [Its] borrowed light never remains in the same state,[27] but grows, weakens, wanes, is brought to nothing and is completely invisible. In a like manner, those who have put their consciences in the mouths of others are now great, then small, and finally nothing at all, according to the preference of flattering tongues for either disparaging or praising [them].

But the sun's splendor is fiery; and as it burns more ardently it even appears brighter to the eyes. Similarly, a wise person's inward burning shines outward, and if both [burning and shining] are not given him, his concern is always to burn more, so that his Father who sees in secret may reward him.[28] Woe to us, brothers, if we have only shone. For we do shine, and are praised[29] by people; but for me, it is a very small thing to be judged by a human tribunal. It is the Lord who judges me,[30] who

16. Is 50:5
17. Ps 84:9 (85:8)
18. Ps 12:4 (13:3)
19. Sg 2:9
20. 2 Co 13:3
21. Is 63:1
22. Ps 50:17 (51:15)
23. Ps 39:10 (40:9)
24. Mk 7:37
25. Jn 5:35
26. Si 27:12
27. Jb 14:2
28. Mt 6:4
29. Lk 4:15
30. 1 Co 4:3-4

requires fervor from everyone, but not splendor. 'I have come,' he says, 'to bring fire to the earth, and what do I will if not that it be kindled?'[31] To be sure, this is a general commandment, this is what is required of everyone; if it happens to be lacking, no excuse is allowed.

4. For the rest, it is especially said to the apostles and to apostolic men: 'Let your light shine before people.'[32] [This is said to them] as to people who have been kindled, and mightily kindled, who are not to fear any situation whatever or the winds' force. It was said even to John, but they hear it in the ear;[33] John, like an angel, is instructed in the spirit. Assuredly, he [was] as close to God as the voice is near the Word. No other voice, which would sound outwardly as an intermediary, was needed for him to be taught.

Inspiration, not preaching, taught John, whom the Spirit filled in his mother's womb.[34] Truly burning and mightily kindled [was] he whom the celestial flame so possessed that he perceived Christ's coming when he could not yet perceive even himself. Surely that new fire, recently fallen from heaven, penetrated the Virgin's ear through Gabriel's mouth,[35] and through the Virgin's mouth and his mother's ear[36] entered into the little child, so that from that moment the Holy Spirit filled his chosen vessel,[37] and prepared a lamp for Christ the Lord.[38] Then he was already a burning lamp, but [he was] still for a time under a bushel, until he could be placed on a lampstand and shine for all who were in the Lord's house.[39] At that time, he was still able to illuminate only his own bushel, and to shine for a while to his mother alone, revealing the great mystery of holiness[40] to her by the motion of [his] singular joy![41]

'Why,' she says, 'does the mother of my Lord come to me?'[42] Who made the Lord's mother known to you, holy woman? 'How do you know me?'[43] 'When the voice of your greeting,' she says, 'came to my ears, the infant in my womb leaped for joy.'[44]

5. Already then he illumined the bushel under which he lay hidden, but the burning lamp under the bushel did not leave hidden the One whom it would soon afterwards make known to the

31. Lk 12:49

34. Lk 1:15

37. Ac 9:15

40. 1 Tm 3:16

43. Jn 1:48

32. Mt 5:16

35. Lk 1:35

38. Ps 131:17 (132:17)

41. Lk 1:44

44. Lk 1:44

33. Mt 10:27

36. Lk 1:41

39. Mt 5:15

42. Lk 1:43

whole world with unheard of brightness. 'He was,' [Scripture] says, 'a burning and shining lamp.'[45] It does not say 'shining and burning,' because John's splendor came from [his] fervor, and not the fervor from [his] splendor. Some do not shine because they are burning, but rather they burn in order to shine: clearly these do not burn with the spirit of charity but with the zeal that comes from vanity. Do you want to know how John both burned and shone?

I think that a threefold [division] can be found in both, that is, in his burning and in his splendor. He was burning in himself with the mighty rigor of his way of life, with the deep and complete fervor of his devotion to Christ, and with the constancy of his bold reproaches to his sinful neighbors. He was shining no less, as I have said briefly, in his example, in pointing out [Christ], in his word; showing himself for the purpose of imitation; greatly illumining what lay concealed for the remission of sins; and for correction, lighting up our darkness, as was written: 'Lord, you who light my lamp, lighten my darkness.'[46]

6. Consider [this] man promised by the angelic annunciation,[47] conceived by a miracle,[48] sanctified in the womb;[49] and marvel at the unheard of fervor of penitence in the new man. 'We have food and clothing,' says the Apostle; 'let us be content with these.'[50] This is apostolic perfection; but John despised even these things. Listen to the Lord in the gospel: 'John the Baptist came,' he says, 'neither eating nor drinking,'[51] and not clothed. For just as the locust is not food, except perhaps for some dumb animals, so neither is camel's hair[52] human clothing. Camel, why did you put aside your hair? Would that you had put aside your hump instead! Why do you dumb beasts and desert reptiles search out delicate foods? John, a holy man, one sent by God[53]— or rather an angel of God, as the Father says: 'Behold, I am sending my angel before you'[54]—John, who was greater than anyone born of women,[55] thus punished, thus weakened, thus afflicted his perfectly innocent body. Do you make haste to dress yourselves in fine linen and purple, and to feast in splendor?[56] Alas! is this all the esteem [you show] this present day? Is this all the reverence

45. Jn 5:35
48. Lk 1:24
51. Mt 11:18
54. Ml 3:1; Mt 11:10

46. Ps 17:29 (18:28)
49. Lk 1:15
52. Mt 3:4
55. Mt 11:11

47. Lk 1:13-17
50. 1 Tm 6:8
53. Jn 1:6
56. Lk 16:19

[you have for] the Baptist? Is this the gladness once prophesied for his birth?[57] Whose memory are you keeping, O overly self-indulgent worshippers? Whose birth are you celebrating? [Is it] not [the birthday] of one who was in the desert roughly clothed, weakened from fasting? 'What did you go out in the desert to see,' children of Babylon? 'A reed shaken in the wind?'[58] What then? 'A man dressed in fine [clothing]'[59] and nourished with fine [food]? All your celebrating revolves around these things: in following the wind of popular favor,[60] in pride in your clothing, and indulgence in food. But why [do] these things for John? John did not act this way, and could never be pleased with such things.

7. 'Many will rejoice at his birth,'[61] the angel says. That is certainly true; many do rejoice at his birth: as we heard, even for pagans [his nativity] is joyous and solemn. They are not aware of what they celebrate, but Christians ought to be. Now Christians do in fact rejoice on blessed John's birthday, but would that they rejoiced because of his nativity and not because of vanity! For what but vanity of vanities[62] is everything under the sun? 'What more does a person have from all the toil with which one toils under the sun?'[63] Brothers, 'under the sun' is everything discerned by the eyes, whatever is seen to lie under this physical light. What is it actually but 'mist appearing for a little while?'[64] What is it but grass and the flower of grass? 'All flesh [is] grass,' says the Lord, 'and all its glory like the flower of grass. The grass withers, and the flower falls, but the word of the Lord endures forever.'[65]

Brothers, let us labor in this word,[66] in which we can live and rejoice forever. Let us work 'not for the food that perishes, but for that which endures to eternal life.'[67] What is that [food]? 'Humankind does not live on bread alone, but on every word that comes from the mouth of God.'[68] Let us sow in this word, dearly beloved, let us sow in the Spirit, because those who sow in the flesh have but corruption to reap.[69] Let us rejoice inwardly, and not under the sun; but, as the Apostle says, 'as if saddened'

57. Lk 1:14   58. Mt 11:7   59. Mt 11:8
60. Livy 22.26.4: *auram favoris popularis*.
61. Lk 1:14   62. Qo 1:2   63. Qo 1:3
64. Jm 4:14   65. 1 P 1:24-25   66. 1 Tm 5:17
67. Jn 6:27   68. Mt 4:4   69. Ga 6:8

from humility and seriousness, 'yet always rejoicing'[70] from inner consolation. Let us rejoice, dearly beloved, on the Nativity of blessed John, and let us rejoice in that very nativity.

8. Our reason for remembering [John] is certainly rich, and the source of [our] rejoicing sundry. 'He was a lamp,' and the Jews were willing to rejoice in his light;[71] [John] rejoiced rather in the fervor of his loyalty: as the bridegroom's friend, he rejoiced in the bridegroom's voice.[72] We are to rejoice in both [ways]: on the one hand for him, and on the other, we are to rejoice together [with him] for ourselves. He burned for himself; he was shining for us. Let us rejoice in his fervor for the purpose of imitation; let us also rejoice in [his] light— yet not remaining there, but that in his light we may see light,[73] the true light, which is not [John] himself, but the One to whom he bears witness.[74]

'John came,' says the Lord, 'neither eating nor drinking.'[75] That is for me an incentive to fervor and a reason for humility. Who among us, brothers, considering John's penitence, can presume, I don't say to boast of his own [repentance], but even to consider it of any importance whatever? Who can venture to grumble during his own labors and say: 'What I am enduring is enough, not to say more than enough'? For what murders, what sacrileges or what disgraceful actions was John thus inflicting punishment on himself? Let us be kindled to penitence, brothers. Let us examine our own consciences, and let us be moved to require chastisement of ourselves, that we may escape the dreadful judgment of the living God.[76] Let the humiliation of a pure confession supply whatever [our] fervor lacks. God is faithful, [77] and if we confess our iniquities, if we set forth our wretchedness, if we do not make excuses for our weaknesses, he will forgive us our sins.[78]

9. After [seeing how John so chastised himself], consider too his fervor with respect to the wrongdoings of [his] neighbors. This order [of things] is certainly fitting and in accord with reason, for remember that you must begin with yourself. 'Cleanse me,' [the psalm] says, 'from my hidden [faults], and spare your servant from the [faults] of others.'[79] 'Brood of vipers,' says John,

70. 2 Co 6:10
71. Jn 5:35
72. Jn 3:29
73. Ps 35:10 (36:9)
74. Jn 1:8-9
75. Mt 11:18
76. Heb 10:31
77. 1 Co 10:13
78. 1 Jn 1:9
79. Ps 18:13-14 (19:12-13)

'who is telling you to flee from the wrath to come?'[80] From what a burning heat of mind do you think those sparks, or rather desolating coals,[81] came forth? Unsparing of the Pharisees he says: 'Do not say, 'We have Abraham for [our] father'; God has the power to raise up children of Abraham from these stones!'[82]

This might seem a small thing, if he had been afraid in the very presence of power, and had not with total freedom of spirit rebuked the sinful, cruel and proud king, coming out of the desert with a kind of holy vehemence for the purpose; or if he had been moved by [the king's] flattering words, or by the fear of death. 'Herod feared John,' [Scripture] says; 'he heard the many things he did, and willingly listened to him.'[83] But [John] spared nothing because of this: 'It is not lawful for you to have her,'[84] he said. Bound and thrust into prison, he stood no less in truth;[85] and he died happily for the sake of truth. May [his] zeal burn brightly in us, dearly beloved; may love of justice burn brightly, [and] hatred of iniquity. Let no one treat vices gently, brothers; let no one pass over sins. Let no one ask: 'Am I my brother's keeper?'[86] Let no one bear calmly what is within him when he sees the Order being lost and discipline weakened. For silence is consent when you are able to rebuke; and we know that a like punishment awaits doers and consentors.[87]

10. What shall we say now about John's humble and completely, exceedingly fervent devotion to the Lord? Because of it he leaped for joy in the womb;[88] because of it he was afraid when he was about to baptize [the Lord] in the Jordan;[89] because of it he said not only that he was not the Christ, as he was thought to be,[90] but even that he was not worthy to loosen the thong of his sandal;[91] because of it the bridegroom's friend rejoiced at the bridegroom's voice;[92] and because of it he said that he had received grace upon grace.[93] People were crying out that he did not have the Spirit by measure,[94] but in the fullness from which all receive.[95] 'Will you not be subject to God, my soul?'[96] But I will not be a burning lamp[97] unless I love the Lord my God with

80. Lk 3:7
81. Ps 119:4 (120:4)
82. Lk 3:8
83. Mk 6:20
84. Mt 14:4
85. Jn 8:44
86. Gn 4:9
87. Rm 1:32
88. Lk 1:44
89. Mt 3:14
90. Jn 1:20
91. Jn 1:27
92. Jn 3:29
93. Jn 1:16
94. Jn 3:34
95. Jn 1:16
96. Ps 61:2 (62:1)
97. Jn 5:35

all my heart, all my mind, and all my strength.[98] That alone is charity which is kindled for salvation; only that which the Spirit infuses and inflames, [the Spirit] we are forbidden to quench.[99] You are informed how John burned, and, if you paid attention, in this was also indicated how he shone. For you would not be able to know his ardor if he had not shone.

11. Therefore, he shone, as I stated above, in his example, in pointing out [Christ], in his word: making himself known by his deed[s], making Christ known by a sign, and making us known to ourselves by his preaching. His father [Zechariah] said: 'You, child, will be called the prophet of the Most High; for you will go before the Lord to prepare his ways, to give knowledge of salvation to his people.'[100] He does not say 'to give salvation,' for he was not the light,[101] but '[to give] knowledge of salvation',' that he might bear witness to the light.'[102]

'[To give] knowledge of salvation,' he says, 'in the forgiveness of sins.'[103] Can a wise person make light of the knowledge of salvation? Yet let us suppose that John has not yet come, that he has not yet pointed out Christ. Where would we seek salvation? I have sinned a great sin which cannot be blotted out by the blood of calves or goats,[104] because the Most High takes no delight in sacrifices.[105] My memory has been stained by these lees and dregs; there is no knife that can scrape this parchment clean, because the whole of it is completely soaked in the dregs. If I should forget my sin, I am foolish and ungrateful; if it remains in my memory, it will reproach me forever. What then shall I do? I will go to John, and listen to the voice of gladness, the voice of mercy, the speech of grace, the word of forgiveness and peace. 'Behold the Lamb of God,' he says, 'behold him who takes away the sins of the world.'[106] In another place he says: 'He who has the bride is the bridegroom.'[107] [John] is revealing that God comes, the Bridegroom, the Lamb. Since [he is] God, it is certain that he can take away sins; but whether he is willing remains a question. Surely he is willing, because he is the Bridegroom, because he is worthy of love. John is the Bridegroom's friend, because the Bridegroom can have none but friends. And although

98. Lk 10:27
101. Jn 1:8
104. Heb 9:19
107. Jn 3:29
99. 1 Th 5:19
102. Jn 1:8
105. Ps 50:18 (51:16)
100. Lk 1:76-77
103. Lk 1:77
106. Jn 1:29

he wants a glorious bride, having no blemish or wrinkle, or any such thing,[108] yet he does not seek such a one—for where would she be found?— but rather he himself makes such a one, such a one as he presents to himself. And then I hear what he says through the prophet: 'It is commonly said,'[109] does a woman, 'if she sleeps with another man,'[110] return to her first husband?[111] 'You have committed fornication with many lovers. Yet return to me, and I will take you back.'[112] Behold what he can do, what he is willing to do.

12. But you may perhaps fear the purification of sins[113] he came to carry out, that with burning and cleaving he may batter bones and bone-marrow, that he may inflict a pain more grievous than death. I have heard: He is a Lamb; he comes in gentleness with wool and milk, making the unholy righteous with his word alone. What, the comic poet asks, is easier than a word?[114] 'Only say the word,' [Scripture] says, 'and my servant will be healed.'[115]

Then why do we hesitate, brothers, and not approach the throne of glory with complete confidence?[116] Let us give thanks to John, and, with him as mediator, let us journey to Christ, because, as [John] says, 'He must increase, but I must decrease.'[117] Decrease in what way? In splendor certainly, not in fervor. He withdrew [his] rays; he gathered himself up, so that he would not be like one who gives forth all his spirit. 'He must increase,' [John] says, the one who can not be emptied, [and] from whose fullness all can receive.[118] 'But I must decrease,' to whom the Spirit has been given by measure,[119] and [to whom] deeds are given so that I may always have strength to burn rather than to shine. I came before the sun, like the morning star; I must be hidden, 'as the sun has risen.'[120] 'I have nothing but a little oil for anointing;'[121] I choose to keep it more safely in a vessel than in a lamp.

---

108. Eph 5:27   109. Jr 3:1   110. Nb 5:13
111. Ho 2:7   112. Jr 3:1   113. Heb 1:3
114. Terence, *Phormio*, 300: *nil est dictu facilius.*
115. Mt 8:8   116. Heb 4:16   117. Jn 3:30
118. Jn 1:16   119. Jn 3:34   120. Mk 16:2
121. 2 K 4:2

the vigil of the apostles peter and paul

THE THREEFOLD AID WE RECEIVE FROM THE SAINTS

ON THE VIGILS OF SAINTS, the spiritual person who desires to celebrate their solemn feasts in spirit and in truth[1] must be vigilant. The vigils [made by] carnal persons differ from those made by spiritual persons. The former make preparations for more splendid services and more sumptuous banquets, and perhaps at those very vigils they perform the works of darkness.[2] 'They rejoice when they have done evil and delight in the worst things.'[3] 'You did not so learn Christ,'[4] you who have followed Christ, who have left everything,[5] who must regard the name of vigils with a vigilant eye. Vigils are appointed for this purpose, that we may be vigilant if we are falling asleep in any sin or in carelessness, and that we may come into the presence of the saints with praise.[6] Not so [are] the children of this world, not so;[7] they are heroes at drinking wine, and valiant men at engaging in drunkeness;[8] they have fallen asleep in their disgrace and their misdeeds. You must know that 'those who are drunk, are drunk at night, and those who sleep, sleep at night,'[9] and the name of holy vigils resounds in vain when these people are more eager to sleep than to be vigilant. But you are not children of the night, nor of darkness, but of light and day,[10] so that the birthdays of the saints will not take you by surprise and find you unprepared.

2. On the feasts of saints there are three things we ought to consider with vigilance: the help that comes from the saint, his example, and our own shame. [We ought to consider] his help, because one who is powerful on earth[11] is more powerful in heaven before the face of the Lord his God. If while living here he had compassion on sinners and prayed for them, now that he knows our miseries more deeply and more truly, he prays to the Father for us. That blessed homeland has not altered his charity but increased it. Because he is wholly passionless, he has not become compassionless; now he has put on heartfelt mercy,[12] as he stands before the source of mercy.

1. Jn 4:23
4. Eph 4:20
7. Ps 1:4; Lk 16:8
10. 1 Th 5:4-5

2. Rm 13:12
5. Mt 19:27
8. Is 5:22
11. Ps 111:2 (112:2)

3. Pr 2:14
6. Ps 94:2 (95:2)
9. 1 Th 5:7
12. Col 3:12

There is another reason which further impels the saints to be concerned about us. According to the Apostle's word, God makes provision for us, that they not be made perfect without us.[13] Thus a saint says: 'The righteous are awaiting me, until you reward me.'[14] We must also consider the example of him who, as long as 'he appeared on earth and lived among humankind,'[15] strayed neither to the right nor to the left,[16] but kept to the king's highway[17] until he came to the One who says: 'I am the way, the truth and the life.'[18] Consider the lowliness of his works, the authority of his words, and then you will see how he shone among humans in word as much as in example, [and] what type of footsteps he left for us, that we may walk by them [and] in them. According to the prophet, 'the path of justice is straight; straight is the road of the just for walking.'[19]

3. But let us give our own shame more careful consideration. That human being, like us, was capable of suffering,[20] fashioned out of the same clay as we were.[21] Why is it, then, that we believe it not only difficult but impossible to perform the deeds he performed, and to follow his footsteps?[22] Let us be ashamed, brothers, and let us quake at this thought, that perhaps this shame may bring glory to us, that perhaps this fear may engender grace in us. There were people who went before us, who traveled life's paths[23] so wondrously that we hardly believe they were human.

In this way, then, on the feasts of saints we ought to rejoice and also be ashamed: [we should] rejoice because we have sent advocates ahead of us; [we should] be ashamed because we cannot imitate them. Thus, our joy in this valley of tears[24] must always be seasoned by the bread of tears,[25] so that grief may always take possession not only of the end of joy, but also of its beginning,[26] Even if the cause for rejoicing is great, greater yet is the cause for sorrow. 'I was mindful of God,' a just one cries out, 'and was delighted'; but at once he adds: ' My spirit failed, I was troubled, and did not speak.'[27]

4. Now if we ought to ponder these things on the vigil of any one of the saints, what shall we do on the solemn feast of the

13. Heb 11:40	14. Ps 141:8 (142:7)	15. Ba 3:38
16. Nb 20:17	17. Nb 21:22	

18. Jn 14:6. Bernard is evidently taking these as words of God the Father.

19. Is 26:7	20. Jm 5:17	21. Jb 33:6
22. 1 P 2:21	23. Ps 15:11 (16:11)	24. Ps 83:7 (84:6)
25. Ps 79:6 (80:5)	26. Pr 14:13	27. Ps 76:4-5 (77:3-4)

greatest and most holy Apostles? I am speaking of Peter and Paul. The feast of one would be enough to spread great rejoicing over the whole earth;[28] but the joining of the two leads to a full measure of joys! 'As they loved each other in life, so in death let them not be separated.'[29] What was more powerful than they while they were on earth? To one the keys of the kingdom of heaven were given,[30] to the other the teaching of the nations.[31] One slays Ananias and Sapphira with the words of his mouth;[32] the other forgives whatever he forgives in the person of Christ,[33] and when he is weakened, then he is stronger, and powerful.[34] How much more powerful are they in heaven who were so powerful on earth![35] Who leave us greater examples than they, who 'in hunger and thirst, in cold and exposure,' and all those things which Paul lists,[36] were continually afflicted, and at last through happy martyrdom ascended together to the heavenly kingdoms. Truly they make us blush for shame,[37] they whom we scarcely dare to look upon, I do not say imitate. Let us beseech them, then, that they may render propitious to us their friend, our Judge, who is God, forever blessed.[38]

---

28. Ps 47:3 (48:2)
29. Antiphon *Gloriosi* once used within the octave of SS. Peter and Paul: cf. 2 S 1:23.
30. Mt 16:19
31. 2 Tm 1:11
32. Ac 5:1-11; Ho 6:5
33. 2 Co 2:10
34. 2 Co 12:10
35. Ps 111:2 (112:2)
36. 2 Co 11:27
37. RB 73:7
38. Rm 9:5

the solemn feast of the apostles peter and paul

Sermon One

THE GLORIOUS SOLEMN FEAST has dawned upon us, [the one] which the splendid martyrs, foremost of the martyrs, princes of the apostles, make sacred by their brilliant death. They are Peter and Paul, two great light-givers,[1] whom God established in the body of his Church as the paired light of [her] eyes.[2] They have been bequeathed to me as teachers [and] mediators to whom I may safely commit myself, because they have shown me the paths of life.[3] With them as mediators, I will be able to rise up to that Mediator who came to make peace through his blood between things in heaven and things on earth.[4]

He is perfectly pure in both his natures, 'he who committed no sin, and in whose mouth no guile was found.'[5] How, then, shall I dare to approach him, I who am a sinner, 'sinning beyond measure,'[6] because my sins are greater than the sands of the sea?[7] He is so pure; is it possible for me to be any more impure? I must fear lest I fall into the hands of the living God,[8] if I presume to draw nigh or cling to him from whom I am separated by a difference as great as the distance between good and evil.

On that account, God has given me these men who were men and sinners, great sinners, who learned in and from themselves how they ought to have compassion on others. Those guilty of great faults will easily pardon great faults, and the amount measured out to them they will return to us.[9] The apostle Peter committed a great sin[10]—perhaps there has been none greater—and pardon followed with equal speed and ease; and in such a way that he lost nothing of his unique primacy. Paul, too, who acted with unique and incomparable violence against the inmost heart of the infant Church,[11] was led to faith by the voice of the very Son of God.[12] As full of good as he had once been of evil, he became a chosen vessel, to bring Christ's name before gentiles and kings and the children of Israel:[13] [He was] a worthy vessel,

---

1. Gn 1:16
2. Ps 37:11 (38:10)
3. Ps 15:11 (16:11)
4. Col 1:20
5. 1 P 2:22
6. Rm 7:13
7. Gn 32:12
8. Heb 10:31
9. Mt 7:2
10. Gn 20:9; see Mt 26: 69-75
11. Ac 9:1-2
12. Ac 9:4-6
13. Ac 9:15

filled with heavenly dishes, from which the healthy can receive food and the sick medicine.

2. It was fitting that such pastors and teachers be appointed for humankind. They would be mild, and mighty, and yet wise. [They would be] mild, that they might receive me gently and mercifully; mighty, that they might strongly protect [me]; wise, that they might lead [me] to the way, and along the way, leading to the city.[14] What is gentler than Peter, who so gently calls all sinners to himself, as the Acts of the Apostles and his pair of letters confirm? What is more powerful than [Peter], whom the earth obeyed when he restored the dead [to life],[15] and under whose feet the sea became something he could tread on?[16] With the spirit of his mouth he reaches Simon the Magician in the air.[17] He receives as his own the keys to the kingdom of heaven,[18] so that the judgment of Peter precedes the judgment of heaven. 'Whatever you have bound on earth,' [Scripture] says, 'will also be bound in heaven, and whatever you loose on earth, will also be loosed in heaven.'[19] And what is wiser than he, to whom a revelation not by flesh and blood is made?[20]

With greatest pleasure I speak next of Paul, who out of goodness beyond measure mourns 'those who have sinned and not repented,'[21] who is stronger than every sovereignty and authority.[22] He brought wisdom and the marrow of holy understanding in abundance, not from the first or second, but from the third heaven.[23]

3. These are our masters, who learned the paths of life[24] thoroughly from the Master of all, and who are teaching us up to the present day. What then have the holy Apostles taught us, or rather do they teach us? Not the fisherman's skill,[25] nor the tent-maker's,[26] nor any other of this kind; not to read Plato, not to interpret Aristotle's subtleties, not to be always learning and never come to knowledge of the truth.[27] They have taught me to live. Do you think that knowing how to live is a small matter? It is a great matter, even the greatest. One who is swollen with pride does not live, nor one defiled by lust, nor one infected with

---

14. Ac 12:10 15. Ac 9:40 16. Mt 14:29
17. Ac 8:18-24; see Nicene and Ante-Nicene Fathers, vol. 8: 484.
18. Mt 16:19 19. Mt 16:19 20. Mt 16: 17
21. 2 Co 12:21 22. Eph 1:21 23. 2 Co 12:2
24. Ps 15:11 (16:11) 25. Mt 4:18 26. Ac 18:3
27. 2 Tm 3:7

other diseases—because this is not living, but disfiguring life and coming near to the gates of death.[28] In my judgment, a good life is to endure evils and to do good, and to persevere in this until death.[29] A popular saying has it that one who feeds himself well, lives well. But 'iniquity has contradicted itself,'[30] for unless one does good, one does not live well.

4. I judge that each one of you who is in [this] community lives well if you live in an orderly, friendly, and humble manner: orderly toward yourself, friendly toward your neighbor, and humbly toward God. [Live] in an orderly way, so that in your whole way of life you are careful to pay heed to your ways, both in God's sight and your neighbor's, guarding yourself from sin, and your neighbor from scandal. [Live] with friendliness, so that you strive to be loved and to love,[31] to show yourself gentle and friendly, to endure not only patiently, but also willingly, the moral and physical weaknesses of your brothers.[32] [Live] with humility, so that when you have done all these things, you may strive to blow away the spirit of vanity, which tends to arise from them, and whenever you perceive it, to totally refuse consent.

So too, in enduring evil which is threefold, you must bring three kinds of foresight. For there are evils which you endure from yourself, from your neighbor, and from God. The first is the austerity of penance; the second, the vexation of others' malice; the third, the scourge of divine correction. In what you endure from yourself, you ought to sacrifice gladly;[33] what is from your neighbor, you ought to bear patiently; what is from God, you ought to endure without grumbling and with thanksgiving.

Not like this are many of the children of Adam, who 'wandered in solitude, in the desert.'[34] Clearly they have wandered, and are wandering, from the way of truth,[35] who, withdrawing into pride's solitude, are unwilling to have a sociable life; in their isolation they cannot be joined. But [they are wandering] 'in the desert' because, moved to no remorseful rain of tears, by their constant dryness they linger in a sterile and parched land. Therefore 'they have not found the way to a city to dwell in'[36] because they have grown old in a foreign land, have shared defilement with the dead, have been reckoned with those in hell.[37]

28. Ps 106:18 (107:18)   29. RB Prol. 50   30. Ps 26:12 (27:12)
31. Augustine, *Confessions*, 2.2: 'Et quid erat, quod me delectabat, nisi amare et amari?'
32. RB 72:5   33. Ps 53:8 (54:6)   34. Ps 106:4 (107:4)
35. Ws 5:6   36. Ps 106:4 (107:4)   37. Ba 3:11

5. That one is not wandering alone, of whom holy Jeremiah says: 'It is good for a man when he bears the yoke from his youth. He will sit alone and be silent, for he has risen above himself.'[38] They have wandered, but he will sit. They always wander in heart;[39] he does not sit, but 'he will sit alone,' when he possesses that singular honor, namely the mark of that judiciary power that the saints will possess in their own land when eternal joy will be theirs. Why [will it be this way]? 'Because he has risen above himself'; that is, although he was a youth, and felt the ardent desires of that unsteady age, he put on the old man, relinquishing what was, and adopting what was not. 'He has risen,' [Scripture] says, 'above himself,' because he did not look at himself, but at the one who is above him. 'He will sit and be silent,' even in the din of devilish suggestions, the din of carnal desires, and the din of the world.

Fortunate is the soul that, although it may hear those tongues, does not listen. More fortunate by far is the soul, if there be any, in whose depths those tongues do not speak. This is the wisdom which the Apostle imparts among the mature, [the wisdom] hidden in mystery, which none of the rulers of this world recognizes.[40] So have the Apostles taught me to live and to set forth. I thank you, Lord Jesus, who ' have hidden these things from the wise and experienced, and revealed them to little children,'[41] to those who have followed you and left everything[42] for the sake of your name.

38. Lm 3:27-28   39. Ps 94:10 (95:10)   40. 1 Co 2:6-8
41. Mt 11:25   42. Mt 19:27-29

[peter and paul]

Sermon Two

THE SAINTS WHOSE SOLEMN MARTYRDOM we celebrate today have provided us with a significant reason for speaking about them, and also with extensive material. I do truly fear one thing: that words of salvation[1] heard so many times may begin to lose their value to us as words. A cheap and changeable thing indeed is a human word, of no space in time,[2] no weight, no value, no solidity. It reverberates in the air[3] (hence we say 'verb'),[4] and, like a leaf caught by the wind,[5] it floats, and there is no one who considers it. Let no one of you, brothers, so comprehend, rather let no one so reprehend the word of God. For I say to you: it would have been good for that man if he had not listened.[6] God's words are the fruits of life, not the foliage; but if [they are] foliage, they are golden. Accordingly, let them not be slighted, not slide away, nor slip by. 'Gather up the fragments, lest they be lost.'[7] Land that has often received a passing rain-shower and not produced fruit is worthless land, near to being cursed.[8] As for the barren fig tree we read about in the gospel,[9] if it was found no less barren after the vineyard-keeper dug and spread dung around it, should not an axe be put to the tree's root?[10]

2. I am telling you that, if the Lord meets with less good among those who dwell in the world, he is going to have greater patience with them than with us, for whom he has reserved an abundant rain of heavenly consolations,[11] and for whom the hoe of discipline has not been lacking, nor the dung of poverty and lowliness.[12] What but dung are the Egyptians' abominations that we sacrifice for our God?[13] Dung [is] clearly worthless to look at, but is useful for producing fruit. Let not one who desires fruitfulness run away from this filthiness! Indeed from an ugly heap of dung that is carried into the field will arise a beautiful heap of sheaves that will be carried from the field. For that reason do not let the precious lowliness appear lowly to you, but reckon

---

1. Ac 13:26   2. 'molis' in 3 MSS   3. 1 Co 9:26
4. This passage is reminiscent of Horace, Epist. I, xviii, 18, 71: 'Volat irrevocabile verbum', cited by Bernard, Pasc 2.9; SBOp 5:99, 17.
5. Jb 13:25   6. Mt 26:24   7. Jn 6:12
8. Heb 6:7-8   9. Lk 13:6-9   10. Lk 3:9
11. Ps 67:10 (68:9)   12. RB 7:49   13. Ex 8:26

reproach suffered for Christ more precious than all Egypt's treasures.[14]

But, for those who own an earthly dung-pit, there is no lack of heavenly rain: it is devoted prayer, pleasant repetition of the psalms, delightful meditation [and] the consolation of the Scriptures.[15] And there is this rain which you receive from my mouth, if, when from the river whose streams gladden the city of God,[16] and the torrent of his delight,[17] some moisture comes to moisten you[18] while we speak about the [Scriptures].

3. But occasionally I am obliged to dig round about, seeing that they have appointed me keeper and dresser in the vineyards. Alas! I who have not cultivated nor kept my own [vineyard][19] am required, as long as I occupy this post, to dig around sometimes and to apply dung.[20] This is a bothersome thing, indeed, but I dare not leave it undone, knowing [as I do] that an axe is much more harmful than a hoe, [and] fire than manure.[21] Thus I have on occasion both to reprove and to chide; I am not unaware that a chiding word, a bitter word, an upbraiding word is like manure: unless excused by necessity, it makes the one uttering it less pleasant. But what do we do when we see that some are enriched with this manure, but others are clearly assaulted and hardened? It has been written: 'An idler shall be assaulted with ox's dung.'[22] Will anyone chided not be enriched, who bears it mildly, responds gently, and willingly attempts to change? Clearly this enrichment is wholesome and fruitful, so that the just one may reproach with mercy and chide: 'Let the oil of a sinner not enrich my head!'[23] From that richness which the sinner's oil produces, thorns and thistles[24] sprout forth more abundantly, and each root of bitterness[25] germinates more plentifully. Thus the one who calls the chiding of the just 'mercy' gives sufficient indication how it ought to be taken, with a mild spirit and faithful mind, and how much gratitude he ought to have. Thus this enrichment will be wholesome for us who receive it, not fruitful in vice like the 'sinner's oil,' but in that result which, according to the Apostle, we possess for sanctification.[26]

14. Heb 11:26
15. Rm 15:4
16. Ps 45:5 (46:4)
17. Ps 35:9 (36:8)
18. Ps 71:6 (72:6)
19. Sg 1:6
20. Lk 13:8
21. Lk 3:9
22. Si 22:2 (Vulg.)
23. Ps 140:5 (141:5)
24. Gn 3:18
25. Heb 12:15
26. Rm 6:22

What then do we do for you, O lazy one, who become more irritated and exasperated on account of this mercy? Have you not spread good manure on your field? Why then does it have stones? But you, O human enemy[27]—since one who loves iniquity hates his own soul[28]—you, I say, human enemy, you have done this, you who are proceeding not to expel your slothfulness but to excuse it; you perversely turn your manure into stones, and are assaulted by what you ought to be enriched by. These things I say, brothers, that you may know how mildly you ought to listen to whatever pertains to the salvation of souls, how devoutly you ought to receive it, and how carefully you ought to guard it, and 'not as the word of humans, but truly as the word of God,'[29] whether it seems consoling,[30] warning, or even chiding. I confess that I have digressed, nearly forgetting this feast, but not to your folly,[31] I think, if these things you have heard adhere firmly to your mind.

4. Now let us try to say something, however brief, about [today's] solemn feast. The day is celebrated as the feast of Christ's Apostles, to whom I know we owe the greatest honor, but whether anyone can show them [honor] I am rather uncertain. For 'your friends have received honor beyond measure, O God; their sovereign power has been strengthened beyond measure.'[32] What then? If while still on earth they were able [to do] all things, not in themselves, of course, but in Christ,[33] what will they not [do] today while living with him in eternal happiness? Still mortal and about to die, they were seen to have power over life and death,[34] bringing death to the living[35] and reviving the dead[36] by their word alone. How much more, now, have they received honor beyond measure, [when] 'their sovereign power has been strengthened beyond measure!'[37]

But what is this, brothers? When today we celebrate the holy memory of the Apostles, are we making a solemn commemoration of their birth or their conversion, of their life or their miracles? [This] is not, brothers, the solemn feast of a human birth, as you recently celebrated the birthday of blessed John. [John]

---

27. Mt 13:27-28   28. Ps 10:6 (11:5)   29. 1 Th 2:13
30. Zc 1:13   31. Ps 21:3 (22:2)
32. Ps 138:17 (139:17), once used as Introit of votive masses of Saint Peter.
33. Ph 4:13   34. Ws 16:13   35. Ac 5:11
36. Ac 9:40   37. Ps 138:17 (139:17)

is honored at his birth because he was born sanctified.[38] Further in John's case alone his birth is more celebrated than his passion, because, although he suffered for Christ when he died for justice and truth, it is more evident that he was born for him, [was] clearly 'a man sent from God,'[39] who was born for this and for this came into the world, to bear witness to the truth.[40] But today we do not remember the Apostles' conversion or their miracles, as on other days, when [Paul's] conversion[41] and [Peter's] liberation from prison by an angel[42] are recalled with the Church's festive expressions of joy. Today their death is more specially honored; nothing among us inspires human thought with more dread than [death].

5. Consider, brothers, the judgment of Holy Church, making her judgment according to faith, not according to appearances.[43] [The Church] recalls the Apostles' death with an especially solemn feast. Today Peter was crucified; today Paul was beheaded: this is the reason for today's feast; this is the cause of our present rejoicing. By making a festive and joyous day on these [anniversaries of death], the Church undoubtedly possesses the spirit of the Bridegroom, the spirit of the Lord, in whose sight, as you find in the psalm, precious is the death of the saints.[44] How many people do we believe were present when the Apostles underwent their sufferings who in no way envied their precious deaths? For 'to the eyes of the foolish they seemed to die, and their going was considered an affliction.'[45] So indeed, 'to the eyes of the foolish they seemed to die': 'But to me,' the prophet says: 'your friends have received honor beyond measure, O God; their sovereign power has been strengthened beyond measure.'[46] Brothers, to the eyes of the foolish, God's friends seem to die, but in the eyes of the wise they are judged instead to be asleep. Lazarus, too, was sleeping, because he was a friend;[47] and 'When he gives sleep to his beloved, behold the heritage of the Lord.'[48]

6. Let us strive, brothers, to live as the just lived, but let us long even more to die as they died. Wisdom reveals the final end of the just,[49] judging us there where she finds us. It is wholly necessary that the end of [our] present life be consistent with the

38. Lk 1:15
39. Jn 1:6-7
40. Jn 18:37
41. Ac 9:1-30
42. Ac 12:3-11
43. Jn 7:24; 2 Co 10:7
44. Ps 115:15 (116:15)
45. Ws 3:2
46. Ps 138:17 (139:17)
47. Jn 11:11
48. Ps 126:2-3 (127:2-3)
49. Ws 2:16

beginning of [our] future life; no difference is tolerable there. As anyone who wants to sew or join together two belts, if I may put it this way, prepares the ends which are to be joined to each other uniformly lest they come apart, and takes little care for the other parts, in a like manner, I say to you, how spiritual a way of life would there be if our ultimate end were carnal, inwardly inconsistent with that spiritual life, for flesh and blood will not be able to possess the kingdom of God?[50] Son, says the wise man, 'remember your final end, and you will not sin.'[51] Because this recollection makes you extremely devout, let fear drive out sin,[52] and not admit negligence.

7. Hence Moses says of some people: 'Would that they be wise, and understand, and provide for [their] final end!'[53] In these words I see three things recommended to us: wisdom, understanding, and prudence. I think that these can be reckoned as three periods of time, so that a certain image of eternity seems to be restored in us: the present for those directing [themselves] by wisdom, the past for those making judgments by understanding; the final end for those thinking ahead with caution. This is assuredly the height of spiritual practice, this a model of spiritual zeal, so that we may wisely dispose our present [life], may reflect on our past in the bitterness of our soul,[54] and may carefully provide for the future. 'Let us,' says the Apostle, 'live soberly, justly and religiously in this world.'[55] So let sobriety be observed in the present; let past times, which have passed away without wholesome results for us, be redeemed with appropriate satisfaction; [and] let us set a shield of godliness against dangers threatening in the future. Godliness, a humble and devout worship of God, alone avails for all things.[56] We are not to provide for the final end in any other way; except that, pondering with unremitting meditation the whole body of dangers which seem to threaten us, we may learn wholly from our own effort to feel more distrust concerning our own merits and to commit ourselves to divine protection alone—with our heart's loving affection and our minds purposeful intention—to the one whose good endowment and perfect gift[57] is a happy and precious death.[58]

---

50. 1 Co 15:50   51. Si 7:40   52. Si 1:27
53. Dt 32:29   54. Is 38:15   55. Tt 2:12
56. 1 Tm 4:8   57. Jm 1:17   58. Ps 115:15 (116:15)

8. You find these three things recommended to you in the gospel by the Lord's own word: 'Blessed are the poor;[59] blessed are the meek;[60] blessed are those who mourn.'[61] Blessed are those with discernment, who with a certain discernment of mind, spit out things present because of an inner desire for those of heaven. Blessed are those who provide for the final end, receiving with meekness the implanted word that can save their souls,[62] and who with a loving heart stretch out toward their future inheritance. Blessed are those who, understanding [their] past error, flood their bed with their frequent tears.[63]

Do you see what the holy man desires, what he longs to obtain for those for whom he prays? He says: 'Would that they be wise, and understand, and provide for their final end!'[64] [It is] as if he were saying with more clarity: Would that the spirits of wisdom and understanding and prudence[65] be present in them! Would that [these spirits] be found in us, brothers, so that we might smoothly arrange all our [affairs] through wisdom, might condemn [our] past sins with understanding, might provide for the future with prudence. Would that we could discern temperance in the present life, that we could understand the amendment of our past life, that we could look forward with devout faith in God in order to have, with God's mercy, a happy end! For this is the threefold cord[66] by which we are drawn to salvation: an ordered way of life, sound judgment, and devout faith.

---

59. Mt 5:3
62. Jm 1:21
65. Is 11:2

60. Mt 5:4
63. Ps 6:7 (6:6)
66. Qo 4:12

61. Mt 5:5
64. Dt 32:29

[peter and paul]

Sermon Three
ON THE READING FROM THE WISDOM BOOK:
THESE ARE MEN OF MERCY

BROTHERS, MOTHER CHURCH rightly attributes to the holy Apostles what we read in the wisdom book: 'These are men of mercy,' and so on.[1] Clearly they are men of mercy, whether they received mercy, were filled with mercy, or were mercifully given to us by God.

Consider the mercy they received. Question Paul about himself, or rather listen [to him] freely confessing: 'I was a blasphemer, and a persecutor, and an unjust man, but I received mercy.'[2] Who has not heard how much evil he did to the saints in Jerusalem?[3] Not only in Jerusalem[4] was he raging, but throughout all of Judaea, to rend the members of Christ on earth. Borne by this fury, he was going [to Damascus], but was prevented by grace. He was going, 'breathing threats and slaughter against the Lord's disciples,'[5] but he too became a disciple of the Lord, and was shown how much he would have to suffer for his name.[6] He set off emitting an awful venom from his entire body, and suddenly was transformed into a chosen vessel,[7] so that his heart might then resound [with] a good word,[8] a loving word, and he could say: 'Lord, what do you want me to do?'[9] Assuredly, 'The right hand of the Most High has changed.'[10] And so he rightfully said: 'The saying is sure and deserving of full acceptance, that the Lord Jesus came to save sinners, of whom I am the foremost.'[11] Brothers, accept this [example] of confidence and consolation in blessed Paul, that, now converted to the Lord, the awareness of [your] past transgressions may not grieve you excessively, but only humble you, as was the case with him who said: 'I am the least of the apostles, unworthy to be called an apostle because I persecuted the Church of God.'[12] Let us be humbled in this way under the mighty hand of God,[13] and let us have

1. Si 44:10   2. 1 Tm 1:13   3. Ac 9:13
4. Translated according to MSS P, CmTd Cl where *et Iudaea* is omitted. Cf. PL 183: 412C.
5. Ac 9:1   6. Ac 9:16   7. Ac 9:15
8. Ps 44:2 (45:1)   9. Ac 9:6   10. Ps 76:11 (77:10)
11. 1 Tm 1:15   12. 1 Co 15:9   13. 1 P 5:6

confidence because we too have received mercy, we have been washed, we have been sanctified.[14] And [Paul's example is] for us all, because we have all sinned and are in need of God's glory.[15]

2. I have another [example], in blessed Peter, to present to you. It is the more precious because it is so rare; and so sublime because of its uniqueness. Paul sinned, but he acted ignorantly in his unbelief;[16] Peter had his eyes open when he fell.[17] 'But where transgression abounded, grace also abounded all the more.'[18] Indeed, for those who sin before they know God, before they experience his compassion, before they carry the gentle yoke and light burden,[19] and before they receive the gift of religion and the consolation of the Holy Spirit,[20] for them, I say, redemption is generous![21] And such were all of us. But of those who, ungrateful for the grace they received, are entangled in sins and vices after their conversion; [who,] having become lukewarm and carnal, look back after putting their hand to the plow;[22] or [who], clearly apostate, go backwards after recognizing the way of truth:[23] of these you will doubtless find a few who after this return to their earlier place[24]—but set in impurities, they are still impure.[25] Over these the prophet weeps bitterly, because 'the gold has tarnished, its fine color has changed;'[26] and 'Those who were brought up in scarlet now are avid for dung.'[27]

3. Yet, if there is anyone like this, let us not lose hope for him so long as he is willing to rise up again quickly. The longer he persists, the more difficult will be his escape. Truly 'blessed is the one who shall take and dash the little ones' of Babylon 'against the rock,'[28] because if they grow up scarcely can they be overcome. 'Little children, I say this, so that you may not sin. But if anyone does sin, we have an advocate with the Father,'[29] who is able to do what we can not in the least do. But let one who has fallen not add to the evil so that he falls more deeply, but rather let him rise,[30] trusting that forgiveness will not be denied him so long as he confesses his sins[31] from his heart.

---

14. 1 Co 6:11   15. Rm 3:23   16. 1 Tm 1:13
17. Nb 24:16   18. Rm 5:20   19. Mt 11:30
20. Ac 9:31   21. Ps 129:7 (130:7) 22. Lk 9:62
23. Tb 1:3   24. Gn 40:13   25. Rv 22:11
26. Lm 4:1   27. Lm 4:5   28. Ps 136:9 (137:8-9)
29. 1 Jn 2:1   30. Am 5:1   31. 1 Jn 1:9

So it was for the one of whom we speak, Peter. After so grievous a fall he attained surpassing holiness. 'He went outside and
wept bitterly'[32]: interpret his going outside as the mouth's confession and his bitter weeping as the heart's compunction. And
notice that then for the first time he remembered the word Jesus
had spoken; then for the first time the word that had foretold
his weakness was present to his heart, when [his] audacious
temerity had lost its strength. Woe to you who show us a more
resolute self after a fall. Why are you so unbending toward your
own destruction? Give way, rather, to be better raised up, and
lest you prevent what has been deformed from being broken so
that it can be better mended. Why are you angered by the cock's
reproach? Be angry at yourself instead. 'O God,' says the psalmist, 'you have reserved an abundant rain for your inheritance,
and it has been weakened.'[33] That is a good weakness which is
reserved for an inheritance, which does not drive away the phy-
sician. He uses an iron rod to dash the hardened to pieces like
a potter's vessel.[34] 'The inheritance has been weakened,' [the
psalm] says; 'but you have strengthened it.'[35]

4. You have heard how our Apostles received mercy, so that
now none of you need be unnecessarily confounded about [his]
past sins, and pricked by them on the bed of his conscience.[36]
Why not? Perhaps you sinned in the world, but did you sin more
extensively than Paul? If you have sinned in the religious life,
did you sin more than Peter? Yet by doing penance with all their
heart they received not only salvation, but also holiness; they even
attained both the ministry of salvation and the magisterium of
holiness. Do likewise[37] then, because Scripture says for your benefit that these were men of mercy.[38] Undoubtedly this was because of the great mercy they were worthy to receive.

5. It is not, however, inappropriate for you to take this phrase
another way: the Apostles were men of mercy, that is, filled with
mercy; or men of mercy, that is, mercifully given to the whole
Church. We know that these men did not live for themselves,
nor did they die for themselves, but for him who died for them;[39]
or rather for all of us on his account. How greatly will their righteousness benefit us when, as has been shown, their sins have

32. Mt 26:75   33. Ps 67:10 (68:9)   34. Ps 2:9
35. Ps 67:10 (68:9)   36. Ps 4:4   37. Lk 10:37
38. Si 44:10   39. 2 Co 5:15

benefitted us so much? Their life, their teaching, even death it-self, works for us: the blessed Apostles have bestowed abstinence on us with [their] conversion, wisdom with their preaching, [and] patience with their suffering. Even today these [men] filled with mercy do not cease from bestowing a fourth [gift], which is the fruit of holy prayers. You may even find something further in their life that you can include, namely, the confidence they offer us by [their] performance of miracles. Who can tell how many benefits have come to us through them? Scripture speaks correctly of them, that 'These are men of mercy'; and it adds: 'whose right-eous works have not been forgotten.'[40]

6. Do you desire that your own [righteousness] not be forgot-ten? Be on guard against a threefold danger, and 'it will flourish forever before the Lord.'[41] You read: 'Because you are lukewarm, I will spit you out of my mouth.'[42] You read: 'If a righteous per-son turns away from his righteousness' and so on, 'I will remem-ber none of his righteous deeds.'[43] You read what is to be said to some at the judgment: 'I do not know you'[44]—doubtless to those who have received their reward.[45] Therefore, all righteous-ness that is lukewarm, all that is transitory, all that is sold, will be forgotten before God.[46] But not so the Apostles' righteous deeds, as appears [clearly] enough from what follows: 'Good things remain with their descendants.'[47] Traces of the Apostles remain for us even today; and their faith, because it is from God, cannot be destroyed.[48] The Israelites' clothes were preserved in-tact during forty years in the desert[49]—How much longer the Apostles' clothes, placed on the Saviour's beast of burden![50]

'With their descendants,' [Scripture] says. What are the descen-dants since there follows: 'the holy inheritance of their children's children'?[51] Surely they are the same, descendants and children's children. You remember, I believe—'I speak to those who know the law—'[52] you remember, I say, the commandment of the law that a surviving brother raise a 'descendant' for his brother who died without a descendant.[53] Who [is] without a descendant? 'I

40. Si 44:10
41. Responsory *Iustus*, once used for the Common of a Confessor not a bishop.
42. Rv 3:16   43. Ezk 18:24   44. Mt 7:23
45. Mt 6:2   46. Lk 12:6   47. Si 44:11
48. Ac 5:39   49. Dt 8:4   50. Mt 21:7
51. Si 44:12   52. Rm 7:1   53. Dt 25:5

am alone,' he says, 'until I pass over'[54]; and upon rising, he says: 'Go, tell my brothers,'[55] as if to say, 'They are [my] brothers; may they act as brothers.' They begot us through the gospel,[56] not however for themselves, but for Christ, because [they begot us] through the gospel of Christ. Hence Paul was troubled because some were called by [the names of] those who had begotten them through the gospel, and he was angry at those who were saying: 'I belong to Paul; I to Cephas; I to Apollos;'[57] he preferred that all be and be called '[belonging] to Christ.' Thus we are the descendants of the Apostles through [their] preaching, but by adoption and inheritance we are the descendants of Christ, and the children's children of the Apostles.

---

54. Ps 140:10 (141:10)   55. Jn 20:17   56. 1 Co 4:15
57. 1 Co 1:12

fourth sunday after pentecost

DAVID AND GOLIATH, AND THE FIVE STONES

WE HAVE HEARD from the Book of Kings[1] about Goliath, a man of great stature, confident on account of his great strength and the immense size of his body, who shouted to the ranks of Israel, challenging them to single combat. We have also heard that God aroused the spirit of a young boy[2] to indignation at [this] spurious and uncircumcized man, who was reproaching the camps of Israel and the armies of the supreme God. We have beheld a mere youth coming forward with sling and stone against an armed man of monstrous bulk, one protected with a shield and helmet and striking terror with other weapons of war. If there were any compassion deep within us, we could not but fear his entering the fight, not but rejoice [with him] at his victory. We have praised the child's strength of spirit, because zeal for God's house consumed his soul, and the insults of those who insulted[3] [God] he did not consider another'. Instead he felt [them] as a personal affront, and he grieved 'over the ruin of Joseph.'[4] We have marveled at such faithfulness in a young man, such [faithfulness] as was not found anywhere in Israel.[5] Finally, we have received all the more joyously the victory granted by heaven and clearly achieved by divine strength, because we have observed apprehensively the combat between a child armed with faith and a giant boasting in his own strength.

2. Now we must consider who this Goliath seems to be, if we are not unaware that the law is spiritual,[6] according to the Apostle's testimony, and was written for us, not only to please us with the appearance of its outer surface, but also to satisfy us with the taste of its inner meanings, as with a kernel of wheat.[7] Elated and inflated by the spirit of his flesh,[8] alone he dared to insult the people of God [who had] already entered the promised land and triumphed over many enemies! I believe that this proud man not inappropriately represents the vice of pride. [Pride] is the greatest sin, because it taunts the people of God to a higher degree, and

1. 1 S 17 2. Dn 13:45 3. Ps 68:10 (69:9)
4. Am 6:6 5. Mt 8:10 6. Rm 7:14
7. Dt 32:14 8. Col 2:18

115

especially rises up against those who seem to have already conquered the other sins. Hence, once the others have been subdued, it challenges to single combat.

At that time, the Philistines were altogether afraid to engage in battle against Israel, save only that all their confidence hung on Goliath, a man of enormous size. Now, for what reason would pride tempt a soul of that kind, one which envy, or the lukewarmness which is wont to cause God to vomit,[9] or the sloth which results in assault by ox's dung,[10] held subject to itself? How, I say, would pride, how would haughty eyes[11] dominate someone whom the other vices dominate to the extent that, as one knowing himself badly, he thinks he is condemned by all? Finally, who but a strong-handed man,[12] one who has already subdued the remaining vices by [his] powerful strength, would come forward to contend against the perfectly vile vice of pride? Let David go forward, I say, strong-handed, because such a great enemy is not conquered except by a strong hand.[13] Let the one who has conquered the bear and the lion[14] arm himself against Goliath!

3. Let him see whether Saul's arm,[15] or secular wisdom and philosophical traditions, or even the surface meaning of divine Scripture which the Apostle calls the written letter that kills,[16] can do him any good. Let him see, I say, whether he is able to vanquish pride with those arms, whether he can lay hold of humility in this way, so that, feeling burdened rather than strengthened,[17] he may toss away arms and baggage of this kind, and cast his pondering entirely on the Lord;[18] and, deeply despairing of his own resources, and armed with faith alone, let him not reflect on Goliath's enormity, lest he perhaps be overwhelmed by the mass of his magnitude, but rather let him sing with his spirit, and sing too with his mind,[19] saying: 'Lord, defender of my life,'[20] and so on. Peter, too, casting himself on the word of the Lord,[21] could not perish or be afraid until[22] he considered the

---

9. Rv 3:16   10. Si 22:2   11. Si 23:5
12. Jos 1:14   13. Ex 13:3   14. 1 S 17:34-35
15. 1 S 17:38-39   16. 2 Co 3:6   17. Ps 54:23 (55:22)
18. 1 S 17:39   19. 1 Co 14:15
20. Ps 26:1 (27:1), as in the Introit formerly used on the Fourth Sunday after Pentecost
21. Lk 5:5
22. Translation assumes a proof-reading error here and reads *donc* as *donec*.

wind's intensity, the sea's depth, and [his] body's weight.[23] But when he saw the strong wind coming he was afraid, and immediately he began to sink[24] because of that very fear.

Likewise, King Saul tries even now to urge something on our champion, saying: 'You are not able to resist this Philistine or fight against him, because you are a boy, and he has been a man of war from his youth.'[25] Nonetheless, [David] did not yield to such a thought but, relying on the strength which had already helped him to win earlier combats[26] he advanced boldy. And so having rejected Saul's arms, he picked up five stones from the stream.[27] Although the stream might sweep away every weightless thing, it could polish these [stones], but not sweep them away with itself. The stream that our soul flows through[28] is, of course, the present world. Scripture testifies that 'a generation comes and a generation passes,'[29] just as a swelling wave pushes in another wave. Since 'all flesh is grass and all its glory like the flower of grass,'[30] the swelling stream easily sweeps along with itself weightless things of this kind; 'but the word of the Lord,' yielding to no billows, 'remains forever.'[31]

4. Accordingly, I think that these five stones are not inappropriately understood as the five kinds of words: of warning, promise, love, imitation, and prayer. Of course an abundance of these words is found everywhere accessible in the sequence of the divine Scriptures. Perhaps these are the very five words Paul mentions, when he prefers to speak five words with understanding than ten thousand in a tongue:[32] 'For the form of this world is passing away';[33] and, according to another testimony, 'The world, and its craving as well, is passing.'[34] As the world passes, these words not only remain but are even made more smooth, just as, with many things passing through, knowledge is manifold.

Now surely David, as he is about to contend with the spirit of pride, is storing those five stones he picked up in the pouch which is his memory, considering how great are God's warnings to us, how much he promises, how great a love he shows us, how many examples of holiness he offers, and, finally, how he recommends to us everywhere earnestness in prayer. Let anyone who is

23. Mt 14:28-30   24. Mt 14:30   25. 1 S 17:33
26. 1 S 17:37   27. 1 S 17:40   28. Ps 123:5 (124:4)
29. Qo 1:4   30. Is 40:6; 1 P 1:24 31. Is 40:8
32. 1 Co 14:19   33. 1 Co 7:31   34. 1 Jn 2:17

hastening to vanquish the vice of pride bear these stones with him, I say, so that as often as the venomous head dares to rise, and whichever of these stones first presents itself to the hand of his thought, Goliath, struck on the forehead,[35] may be cast down, covered with shame. A sling, in the shape of long-suffering, is also clearly necessary in this conflict. For no reason can it be absent from this combat.

5. As often as the thought of vainglory agitates [your] mind, if from your heart's deepest inclination you begin to fear the divine warnings, or to long for [God's] promises, Goliath will not withstand the blow of either of these stones, but every swelling will be immediately checked. If such an ineffable love as God's majesty[36] showed you comes into your mind, do you not immediately, as you take fire with charity, begin straightway to abominate and abandon vainglory? Thus, too, if you put the examples [given by] the saints before you for your careful consideration, this very useful thought will undoubtedly serve to check [your] self-exaltation. Moreover if perhaps, as self-exaltation suddenly arises, your hand cannot take hold of any of these [stones] we have mentioned, turn with all fervor toward what alone remains, prayer, and immediately the one whom you had seen elevated and exalted like the cedars of Lebanon, [this] ungodly one, having been overthrown, will be no more.[37]

6. But perhaps you are asking how you may be able to cut off Goliath's head with his own sword?[38] That [would be] the more agreeable to you as it would be more grievous to the enemy. I shall be brief since I speak to the experienced, and they grasp easily and remark without delay what they perceive repeatedly acted out within themselves. As often as, at vainglory's challenge, you begin to be ashamed and to blush at the remembrance of the divine warning, or promise, or the other [stones] we spoke of above, Goliath has indeed been cast down, but is perhaps still living. So come up closer, lest perhaps he rise up again; and, standing over him, cut off his head with his own sword's point, destroying vainglory with the very vainglory that assails you. You have slain Goliath with the sword of Goliath if, struck by that haughty thought, from it you take the material and occasion for humility, regarding yourself henceforward as humbly and abjectly as [you regard] that proud man.

35. 1 S 17:49   36. Ps 28:3 (29:3)   37. Ps 36:35-36 (37:35-36)
38. 1 S 17:51

sixth sunday after pentecost[1]

Sermon One
ON THE GOSPEL READING WHERE THE CROWD, REMAINING WITH THE LORD FOR THREE DAYS, IS FED WITH SEVEN LOAVES OF BREAD[1]

'**I** have compassion on the crowd, because they have remained with me for three days now, and have nothing to eat.'[2] Brothers, the gospel was written for this purpose, and it is to be read for no other reason than this, that we obtain from it spiritual consolation and desolation. A profusion of material things is an empty consolation for people in the world, [and] a scarcity of them is a desolation no less empty. But the gospel, the mirror of truth, flatters no one, misleads nobody. Whoever finds himself [in the gospel] such as he is, will be the sort of person who does not falter with fear where no fear exists,[3] nor rejoice when he does evil.[4]

But what does Scripture say? 'If anyone is a hearer of the word and not a doer, this person will be compared to a man looking at the face of his birth in a mirror. For he looked at himself, and went away, and at once forgot what he was.'[5] Yet I beseech you, brothers, not [to be] like this, not like this[6]: but in [the light of] that reading we heard from the holy gospel, let us examine ourselves, that we may benefit from it, and in its spirit amend whatever we may detect in ourselves to be amended. On account of this, the prophet chooses that his ways be directed toward keeping the Lord's ordinances.[7] 'Then,' he says, 'I will not be put to shame when I have fixed my eyes on all your commandments.'[8]

And indeed I am not put to shame.[9] Instead I boast about you,[10] my brothers, because after following the Saviour in the desert, you have gone forth to him outside the camp.[11] But I fear that perhaps someone may be found irresolute during that three day wait, and return to the Egypt[12] of this dissolute world[13] in heart or even in body. Accordingly, divine Scripture justifiably calls

1. Mk 8:1-9
2. Mk 8:2
3. Ps 13:5 (14:5)
4. Pr 2:14
5. Jm 1:23-24
6. Ps 1:4
7. Ps 118:5 (119:5)
8. Ps 118:6 (119:6)
9. Ga 4:20
10. 2 Co 9:2
11. Heb 13:13
12. Nb 14:3-4
13. Ga 1:4

out and says: 'Wait for the Lord, act bravely, let your heart take courage, and remain with the Lord.'[14] But how long must you remain? Plainly, until he has compassion on you.[15] Do you ask when he will have compassion? 'I have compassion,' he says, 'on the crowd, because they have remained with me for three days now.'[16]

2. It is necessary that you undertake a three-day journey[17] in the desert if you wish to offer a pleasing sacrifice to your God, and that you remain with the Saviour for three days if you desire to be filled with the loaves of the miracle. The first is the day of fear: a day, I say, that manifests and lightens your darkness,[18] inner [darkness], that is, and reveals the dreadful punishment of hell, in which outer darkness[19] exists. Reflection of this kind is, as you yourselves know,[20] wont to provoke the beginning of our conversion. The second is the [day] of holiness, by which we are refreshed in the light of God's compassion.[21] The third is the day of reason, in which truth becomes known, so that as from a certain obligation of nature, without any opposition, creation is subjected to the Creator, [and] the servant serves the Redeemer.

Hereupon we are ordered to sit down,[22] that charity may be set in order in us.[23] Hereupon the Lord opens his hand, and fills every creature with [his] blessing.[24] But because it is said to the apostles: 'Have the people sit down,'[25] even though it perplexes me, you have deputies of whatever sort, of whom I am one, who urge you to sit down, dearly beloved, so that being refreshed by the bread of blessing, you may be able to continue on the way and that you may not, forced by wretched necessity, go down, you too, into Egypt,[26] and those who have not yet followed the Saviour into the desert with you may not begin to mock you.[27] Wretched are those too who have not gone forth with those going forth; but clearly more wretched than all humanity[28] are those who have set forth with the others, but have not been refreshed along with them.

14. Ps 26:14 (27:14)   15. Ps 122:2 (123:2)   16. Mk 8:2
17. Ex 3:18   18. Ps 17:29 (18:28)   19. Mt 8:12
20. Translated as *nostis* instead of *nostris*, which seems to be a mistake in proofreading. Cf. PL 183: 337D.
21. Si 36:1   22. Mk 8:6   23. Sg 2:4 (Vulgate)
24. Ps 144:16 (145:16)   25. Jn 6:10   26. Gn 43:15
27. Lk 14:29   28. 1 Co 15:19

3. Furthermore, if there were some who lay concealed, hidden behind thornbushes or a shelter of any kind whatever, while the others were sitting, who does not know that persons of this kind remained hungry[29] and empty? No less [was this] so for those wandering about every which way, led by levity and curiosity, who scarcely sat down at all, or who did in fact sit down but not in order or in the number of the others.[30]

Accordingly, we encourage your charity, and warn you with pastoral concern, that none of you be found to love nooks, to frequent hiding places, to seek out of the way places, for 'one who does wrong hates the light and does not come to the light lest his deeds be exposed.'[31] But neither should any be found among you who are carried about by every wind of doctrine,[32] unstable and unsettled, having neither solidity nor weight, 'like the dust that the wind sweeps from the face of the earth.'[33] And what shall I say of those whose hand [is] against everyone, and everyone's hand against them?[34] 'These are the ones who separate themselves, worldly people, devoid of the Spirit'[35] because 'no one speaking in the Spirit of God says "Jesus be cursed!" '[36] Clearly this bane is extremely harmful and destructive, because the obstinacy of one person disturbs everyone and becomes the cause of discord, the material of scandal, for all. Finally, I listen to the prophet who, speaking about the Lord's vineyard says: 'Each wild beast has devoured it.'[37] For [reasons] of this kind, I ask and beseech you, my brothers: flee all deceit and the nooks of your own will; flee restlessness and the spirit of levity. Flee obstinacy and the extremely harmful vice of aloofness—unless perhaps, which God forbid, you want to rob your souls[38] of the food of blessed bread.

4. Now lest I detain you any longer,[39] these are the seven loaves[40] by which you are to be refreshed. The first loaf is the word of God in which is a person's life, as he himself testifies.[41] The second loaf is obedience, because 'My food,' he says, 'is to do the will of the one who sent me.'[42] The third loaf is holy meditation, about which was written: 'Holy reflection will preserve

29. Mk 8:3
32. Eph 4:14
35. Jude 19
38. Qo 4:8
41. Mt 4:4

30. Mk 6:39-40
33. Ps 1:4
36. 1 Co 12:3
39. Ac 24:4
42. Jn 4:34

31. Jn 3:20
34. Gn 16:12
37. Ps 79:14 (80:13)
40. Mk 8:5

you';[43] and likewise it seems to be called elsewhere the bread of life and understanding.[44] The fourth loaf is the tears of those who pray. The fifth is the labor of repentance. You should not wonder that I speak of labor and tears as bread unless perhaps you have forgotten what you read in the prophet: 'You will feed us on the bread of tears';[45] and again in another psalm: 'Because you will eat the labors of your hands, you are happy and it will be well with you.'[46] The sixth loaf is pleasant social concord: a loaf, let me say, baked from diverse grains,[47] and assuredly leavened with God's wisdom. Finally the seventh loaf is the Eucharist, 'The loaf,' [Christ] says, 'that I give you is my flesh for the life of the world.'[48]

43. Pr 2:11   44. Si 15:3   45. Ps 79:6 (80:5)
46. Ps 127:2 (128:2)   47. 1 Co 10:17   48. Jn 6:51

[pentecost six]

Sermon Two
THE FRAGMENTS [WHICH ARE] THE SEVEN MERCIES

DO YOU KNOW WHAT I have done[1] by setting seven works of mercy before you today? I have distributed seven loaves of bread.[2] Now if day and night my tears have become my bread,[3] how much more the divine compassion? For it tastes far sweeter, is much more refreshing, and more fully strengthens the human heart.[4] Unless I am mistaken, many mouthfuls from these loaves[5] have fallen to us today. While I was breaking [the loaves], I felt many morsels escape from [my] hands and slip between [my] busy fingers: you will see whether you gather any of them. If you do not yet shrink from it, I will impart ungrudgingly[6] the pieces that I gathered for myself lest perhaps I incur the curse of one hoarding grain among the people.[7] The first loaf, if I remember well, was the saving [power] of grace; it kept me, although unworthy, from many sins while I was still in the world. I hold the three fragments of this [loaf], a possession [containing] great delight to the taste[8] and support to life. Indeed, I remember that I was preserved from sin in three ways: by removal of the occasion, by strength given [me] to resist, and by healing of the inclination [to sin]. I might easily have fallen into many sins if the occasion had been presented; but through God's compassion, no such opportunity took hold of me. Into many, too, I would have fallen nearly as much, severely driven by the violence of temptation. But the Lord, king of virtues,[9] gave [me] virtue[10] so that my desire would be subject to me,[11] and so that I would not consent to the craving I felt. But your compassion, Lord, made me so distant from those [sins], that I inwardly despised them, and not one temptation to them bothered me.

2. The second loaf was the awaiting by which [God] put off vengeance because he was pondering forgiveness. Receive the three fragments of this loaf, too, as you ponder the forbearance which he displayed, the choice of his predestination which he

1. Jn 13:12	2. Mk 8:6	3. Ps 41:4 (42:3)
4. Ps 103:15 (104:15)	5. Mk 8:8	6. Ws 7:13
7. Pr 11:26	8. Ws 16:20	9. Ps 67:13 (68:12)
10. Ps 67:36 (68:35)	11. Gn 4:7	

willed to be fulfilled, and the charity beyond measure with which he loved me.[12] On account of this, the waiting Lord awaited us,[13] and did not turn his attention toward me but turned his eyes away from my sins,[14] as if not wanting to notice how much I had transgressed.[15] On account of this, I say, he kept silent to commend his patience, to fulfill his choice, [and] to confirm his charity.

3. Concerning the third loaf, namely his mercy by which he turns us to repentance, I set before you not so much mouthfuls as morsels. Then, as I remember well, he struck my heart, arousing it to notice the wounds of its sins and to feel the pain of [its] wounds. He even terrified [me], leading [me] down to the gates of hell,[16] and showing [me] the punishments made ready for the unjust. And that no harmful pleasure might remain, breathing a better consolation into me, he gave me hope of forgiveness. By these three [morsels] then I was converted, and I believe that you [were], too.

4. Now the fourth loaf is that forgiveness itself. I beseech you, gather up the fragments carefully, that they not be lost.[17] They are exceedingly wholesome, and sweeter than honey and the honey-comb.[18] So completely did he forgive me and so lavishly did he pardon every wrong, that now he neither condemns me to punishment, nor shames me with reproaches, nor loves me less because of his reckoning. There are some who so forgive a wrong that they do not punish, but yet offer frequent reproaches. There are others who keep silent, even when a proud thought is stored away in their minds:[19] they retain bitter thoughts in the heart. Certainly, neither of these is complete forgiveness.

Far from all these is God's perfectly kind nature. He acts lavishly, he forgives fully, so that on account of the confidence of sinners, repentant ones, where wrong-doing abounded, grace may be wont to abound all the more.[20] Paul, teacher of the gentiles, is a witness: he, more than all the others, labored with divine grace.[21] Matthew is also a witness: chosen as an apostle from

---

12. Eph 2:4   13. Ps 39:1 (40:1)   14. Ps 50:11 (51:9)
15. Ws 11:24   16. Ws 16:13; Is 38:10   17. Jn 6:12
18. Ps 18:11 (19:10)
19. The latin text... *manet tamen alta mente repositum* is translated according to MSS Cl and Cl', *reposita* and *reposta* respectively. Cf. PL 183: 342CD. That translation assumes agreement between a neuter plural subject and a singular verb, common in earlier medieval Latin.
20. Rm 5:20   21. 1 Co 15:10

the customs house,[22] it was given him to be the first writer of the New Testament. Peter, too, is a witness: to him, after his triple denial,[23] was entrusted the pastoral care of the entire Church.[24] Finally, even that very notorious female sinner attests [to this];[25] at the very beginning of her conversion, what a great love was bestowed on her, and later what a forgiving grace of intimate acquaintance! Who accused Mary [Magdalene] , and was it necessary for her to defend herself?[26] When a Pharisee grumbles, when Martha complains,[27] [and] when the Apostles are scandalized,[28] Mary keeps silent. Christ excuses her and even praises her silence. And last, how great a privilege, how great a distinction was it, that she was worthy to be the first to see, the first to touch [him] risen from the dead![29]

5. Now let us go on to the other loaves. Indeed it is good for us to be here,[30] where confidence is given to sinners; but I must not keep silent about the remaining loaves. In abstinence, which is the fifth loaf, I also find three [fragments]. Whence I may justly proclaim: 'The Almighty has done great things for me!'[31] Perhaps you consider your abstinence a small matter; but I do not. I know what opponents it may have, and how much strength it needs to be able to resist them. The flesh lusting against the spirit[32] is, of course, the first enemy of our abstinence. What an enemy within our own household,[33] what a perilous struggle, what an internal war! O my soul, we can neither flee this cruelest enemy nor put it to flight. We must carry it around with us, because it is bound to us. Now, what is more perilous and wretched: we ourselves are compelled to sustain our enemy, and are not permitted to slay it? You see then how carefully you must protect yourself from what sleeps in your bosom.[34]

Nonetheless, this is not my only adversary; I have yet another which surrounds and beseiges me from all sides. If you do not know, this enemy is the present wicked age.[35] The enemy has blocked my ways,[36] and with his darts he wounds me through five gates—[my] body's five senses—and death enters through my windows.[37]

22. Mt 9:9
23. Mt 26:69-74
24. Jn 21: 15-17
25. Lk 7:36-50
26. Lk 7:39
27. Lk 10:40
28. Mt 26:8-9
29. Jn 20:14-17
30. Mt 17:4
31. Lk 1:49
32. Ga 5:17
33. Mi 7:6; Mt 10:36
34. Mi 7:5
35. Ga 1:4
36. Lm 3:9
37. Jr 9:21

These two [adversaries] were more than enough. But, woe is me! Behold, I see a strong wind[38] coming from the north, from which every evil spreads out.[39] And now what other thing remains? 'Lord, save us, we are perishing!'[40] For see the hammer of the whole earth;[41] see the serpent, more cunning than all other living things;[42] see that foe whom I cannot see, much less guard against! For the struggle of those wanting to preserve abstinence—I do not mean abstinence from dissipation alone, but also from the other vices and sins, as required— their 'struggle is not against flesh and blood alone , but against the princes and powers, against the world rulers of this present darkness, against the spiritual [hosts] of wickedness in the heavens.'[43] Who can extinguish their fiery darts?[44] 'They made their arrows ready in the quiver, to shoot in the dark at the upright in heart';[45] but also 'They spoke of hiding their snares, and they said: Who will see them?'[46] They assail and pursue us, sometimes openly and violently, sometimes secretly and deceitfully, but always wickedly and cruelly. Who is capable of tolerating, much less of overcoming them?

I believe that the difficulty of abstinence is now sufficiently well known to you, so that, as the Apostle says, you may know what God has bestowed on you.[47] For wholly in God we do valiantly, and he leads our oppressors to naught.[48] He it is who crushes under our feet[49] not only our flesh with its self-indulgent desires,[50] but also the present evil age[51] with its inquisitiveness and emptiness, and even Satan himself[52] with his temptations. Now have I not spoken worthily of what is to be found in abstinence? Hence I proclaim: 'The Almighty has done great things for me!'[53]

6. Now accept the fragments of the sixth loaf. This loaf is the grace of deserving, [deserving] the good things of eternal life. I believe this gift consists especially of three things: hatred of past evils, contempt of present goods, and the desire for future goods.

The seventh loaf is the hope of obtaining; I have no less than three mouthfuls from it, too, and their taste [is] very sweet to my palate.[54] There are three, I say, which so strengthen and em-

38. Mt 14:30   39. Ezk 1:4; Jr 1:14   40. Mt 8:25
41. Jr 50:23   42. Gn 3:1   43. Eph 6:12
44. Eph 6:16   45. Ps 10:3 (11:2)   46. Ps 63:6 (64:5)
47. 1 Co 2:12   48. Ps 59:14 (60:12)   49. Rm 16:20
50. Ga 5:24   51. Ga 1:4   52. Rm 16:20
53. Lk 1:49   54. Sg 2:3

bolden my heart that I am firmly established in them and cannot be cast down from hope's height by any want of merits, any consideration of my own lowliness, any estimation of the value of heavenly happiness. Do you desire these [mouthfuls], or should they be put aside, because of him who said: 'Have you found honey? Eat only enough for you'[55]? What wisdom prophesied about herself is fulfilled today—and now I see that very [thing]—because 'Those who eat me,' she says, 'will still be hungry.'[56]

Accordingly, I shall not detain you any further, but neither shall I defraud you of your hunger, because I see you prepared as if you had not yet received anything. I am thinking of three things in which all my hope consists: the charity of [my] adoption [by God], the truth of [God's] promise, the power of keeping [it]. Let my foolish pondering complain now as much as it wishes, and say: Who are you? And how great is that glory? And by whose merits do you hope to obtain it? And I shall answer with confidence: I know him in whom I have believed,[57] and I am certain that he adopted me in his exceedingly great love,[58] that [he is] true in his promise-making, that [he is] powerful in his delivering; for he can do what he wills. This is 'the threefold cord' which 'is broken with difficulty,'[59] which has been let down for us from our homeland into this prison. Let us grasp it firmly, I beseech you, so that it can lift us up, that it can draw us, draw us all the way to the vision of the glory of our great God,[60] who is forever blessed.[61]

---

55. Pr 25:16   56. Si 24:29   57. 2 Tm 1:12
58. Eph 2:4   59. Qo 4:12   60. Tt 2:13
61. Rm 9:5

[pentecost six]

ON THE OCCASION OF THE PRECEDING SERMON
THE HEART'S LOFTINESS AND BASENESS

Of what was just said, that some look up and others down, I have something further which I should not refuse to speak to your charity. Of the thoughts we expressed then, if you remember well, though one may be more perfect both are nonetheless useful. There are some who may hold their heart in another way or upwards, as God made humans upright,[1] and they can respond with confidence to the priest who is exhorting them: 'We have lifted them up unto the Lord.'[2] There are others who, bending downwards with the dumb animals, cause themselves to be mocked by impure spirits who cry out in derision: 'Bow down that we may pass over you.'[3]

You know that in a community of many it is impossible for all to be of the same strength, either in body or in character, and so the authority of our Rule advises [us] to bear each weakness with patience,[4] and charity requires [us] to stoop down somewhat to each. Some other person sees this, and perhaps he begins to envy one whose pain he ought to share. Hence it happens that often in his heart he calls that person happy on account of the thing for which he should count him wretched, bearing his own need with difficulty. Therefore, he proves that he is altogether bowed down and has his mind set on the flesh with a base heart: with him wretchedness itself is not without envy. When the superior grants them dispensations out of a certain consideration of charity for another's need, he sets his heart[5] on such things. He seeks similar things [and] grumbles about the one who turns him down when he makes his request unreasonably. Hence suspicions are stirred up, and slander and scandals.

2. I do not say this, dearly beloved, as if I have anything particularly to complain about concerning you on this matter. But I considered it necessary to forewarn and fortify you beforehand, because many among you are tender and delicate, and for them, either age or infirmity requires some moderation of the rigor of [our] common rule. [Give] thanks to the one from whose gift it

1. Qo 7:30   2. Preface to the Eucharistic Prayer   3. Is 51:23
4. RB 72.51   5. Ps 61:11 (62:10)

comes that I see many here whose minds are intent on God, and who have become so distant from that base thought that they are completely unaware that the weaker ones near them complain to every one that they do less. Undoubtedly those in higher places are always heedful, with the Apostle having forgotten what lies behind and straining forward to what lies ahead.[6] How greatly do I wonder at them, do you think? How much reverence do I have for them in my heart? With how much loving feeling do I embrace them? As if not knowing those whom they see in their company daily, they choose for themselves out of them all one or perhaps two, or even more, whom they see in greater fervor of spirit; and although they themselves may perhaps be more perfect, yet they always propose and purpose for themselves their holy zeal in the Lord, and their physical and even spiritual practices.

3. I remember that I have already said [this] on another occasion, but I will not consider it burdensome to repeat how a certain lay monk once gave himself to the loftiest meditation during the entire period of vigils. Very early in the morning he took hold of me, and drawing me into the speaking room said, prostrate at my feet: 'Woe is me! I considered a single monk in my vigils; I counted thirty virtues in him, and do not find even one of them in myself!' Perhaps he possessed none as great as was this humble attitude of holy rivalry. Let this be the fruit of our sermon: that you be always mindful of higher things, because the fullness of humility consists of that. Perhaps the grace bestowed on you on a certain count seems greater [than that given] some other brother, but if you are a zealous rival[7] you will be able to judge yourself inferior on many counts. What if you are able to work or fast more than he, but he surpasses you in patience, outstrips you in humility, and towers above you in charity? Why do you meditate in foolish thought all day about what you seem to have? Be more concerned to know what you are lacking![8] This is better. Brothers, would that we were as desirous of spiritual grace, as people of the world are of the money which passes. Certainly we have the duty, an important duty, to vanquish evil with good;[9] and to desire all the more fully as what we desire is more precious. If only we could all be equal! Great is the disorder, exceed-

6. Ph 3:13   7. 1 P 3:13   8. Ps 38:5 (39:4)
9. Rm 12:21

ingly great, in that they desire what is destructive more ardently than we desire what is useful. They hasten more quickly toward death than we do toward life. For who can express how greatly a miser is tortured by his desire for money, how greatly an ambitious man seethes with his craving for honor, and finally, how impetuously 'each one is drawn on by what delights him.'[10] You can see that they care little for whatever they have obtained, that they do not pay attention to what they were scarcely able to acquire at last with such great effort and longing. Everything becomes worthless to them before their desire for some perhaps lesser thing, which they have begun to envy someone else.

4. And you, then, must not reflect very much on what you may seem to possess, except perhaps occasionally. This is so that you can give thanks and acknowledge yourself a debtor to him who gave it, whether out of the grace of consolation, when it is necessary, or so that you may not be saddened for any reason whatever. For the rest, always be more mindful of what another possesses [and] you do not, because this thought preserves you in a humble state and distances you from a falling off into lukewarmness; but even more, it also enkindles in you a desire for improvement. See, on the contrary, how many evils are produced by that reflection in which you busily turn over in your mind what you appear to yourself to have, and what you reckon someone else does not have. Hence when you put yourself before another you are raised to pride; when you judge yourself someone great you neglect to improve; when in comparison to another you seem to have done too much, just then you begin to fall away; and in this way, you fall into lukewarmness and begin to act with more slackness. We know 'that God opposes the proud but gives grace to the humble,'[11] and that 'one who does the Lord's work negligently is cursed.'[12] But 'blessed are those who hunger and thirst for righteousness,'[13] because if by the Spirit we have put to death the deeds of the flesh we will live, [but] if we have lived according to the flesh we will die.[14]

---

10. Virgil, *Eclogues*, II, 65   11. 1 P 5:5   12. Jr 48:10
13. Mt 5:6   14. Rm 8:13

aBBReviations¯

The standard abbreviations used by the Jerusalem Bible are employed for the books of the Bible. For the Psalms, the first number indicates the number in the Vulgate and the second, the number in the Jerusalem Bible.

The translation itself and references to other Bernardine texts are based on Sancti Bernardi Opera (SBOp), the critical edition in nine volumes, edited by Jean Leclercq, Henri Rochais and C.H. Talbot, and published by Editiones Cistercienses in Rome between 1957 and 1977.

ABBREVIATIONS FOR THE WORKS OF SAINT BERNARD

Adv	Sermo in adventu Domini
AltBasCor	De altitudine et bassitudine cordis
Asc	Sermo in ascensione Domini
Csi	De consideratione libri v
Div	Sermones de diversis
JB	Sermo in nativitate Ioannis Baptistae
Pent	Sermo in die sancto Pentecostes
IV p P	Sermo in dominica quarta post Pentecosten
VI p P	Sermo in dominica sexta post Pentecosten
PP	Sermo in festo SS. apostolorum Petri et Pauli
QH	Sermo super psalmum Qui habitat
SC	Sermo super cantica canticorum
VPP	Sermo in vigilia apostolorum Petri et Paul

OTHER ABBREVIATIONS USED IN THIS VOLUME

ASOC	*Analecta Sacri Ordinis Cisterciensis*
CF	Cistercian Fathers Series
Cîteaux	*Cîteaux: Commentarii Cistercienses*
Coll	*Collectanea Ordinis Cisterciensium Reformatorum*
CS	Cistercian Studies Series
CSt	Cistercian Studies
PL	J.-P. Migne, *Patrologiae cursus completus*, series latina. 221 volumes. Paris, 1844-64.
RB	*Regula monachorum sancti Benedicti (Rule of St Benedict)*

sUBJECT inδex

scRiptuRal inöex

Column one indicates the scriptural book with its abbreviation and the verses cited. Column two indicates the abbreviation for the Bernardine sermon with the section number corresponding to the paragraph divisions in the Latin edition.

Genesis (Gn)

1:16	PP 1,1
1:26	Asc 4,5
2:4	Pent 2,4
3:1-6	Pent 2,3
3:1	VI p P 2,5
3:5	Asc 4,5
3:15	Asc 4,4
3:18	PP 2,3
4:7	VI p P 2,1
4:9	JB, 9
5:22	Asc 6,9
5:24	Asc 3,2
6:3	Asc 3,8
11:4-9	Asc 4,5
16:12	VI p P 1,3
20:9	PP 1,1
23:4	Asc 3,6
26:27	Rog 1,1
27:28	Pent 2,6
28:12	JB, 1
28:17	JB, 1
32:12	PP 1,1
40:13	PP 3,2
41:41	Asc 3,2
43:15	VI p P 1,2

Exodus (Ex)

3:18	VI p P 1,2
7:12	Asc 3,9; Asc 6,11
8:26	PP 2,2
13:3	IV p P, 2
19:14	Asc 4,6

Psalms (Ps) The first number indicates the number in the Vulgate,
and the second the number in the Jerusalem Bible.

1:2	Asc 6,7
1:4	VPP, 1; VI p P 1,1; VI p P 1,3
2:9	PP 3,3
4:3 (4:2)	Asc 4,4; Asc 4,8
4:4 (4:3)	Asc 4,8; Asc 4,9
4:4	PP 3,4
4:7	Pent 2,6
6:7 (6:6)	PP 2,8
8:2 (8:1)	JB, 1
9:24 (10:3)	Asc 4,3
9:38 (10:17)	Asc 5,2
10:3 (11:2)	VI p P 2,5
10:6 (11:5)	Rog 1,1; PP 2,3
12:4 (13:3)	JB, 2
13:5 (14:5)	VI p P 1,1
15:11 (16:11)	Asc 2,2; Asc 4,7; VPP, 3; PP 1,1; PP 1,3
17:12 (18:11)	Pent 1,1
17:29 (18:28)	JB, 5; VI p P 1,2
18:6 (19:5)	Asc 4,7; JB, 1
18:7 (19:6)	Asc 3,1; Asc 4,7; Pent 3,8
18:11 (19:10)	VI p P 2,4
18:13-14 (19:12-13)	JB, 8
18:15 (19:14)	Asc 4,7
20:4 (21:3)	Asc 6,14
21:3 (22:2)	Asc 6,14; PP 2,3
21:18 (22:17)	Asc 4,6
21:25 (22:24)	Asc 5,1
22:6 (23:6)	Pent 2,7
23:3 (24:3)	Asc 4,6
23:7-10 (24:7-10)	Asc 2,4
24:8 (25:8)	Pent 3,6
24:11 (25:11)	Pent 2,3
24:13 (25:13)	Asc 4,8
24:15 (25:15)	Asc 4,7
25:3 (26:3)	Pent 2,7
26:1 (27:1)	IV p P, 3
26:6 (27:6)	Asc 4,9
26:8 (27:8)	Asc 4,7

50:17 (51:15)	JB, 2
50:18 (51:16)	JB, 11
53:8 (54:6)	PP 1,4
54:7 (55:6)	Asc 4,8
54:9 (55:8)	Pent 1,2
54:15 (55:14)	Asc 3,6
54:23 (55:22)	IV p P, 3
57:4 (58:3)	Pent 2,3
58:11 (59:10)	Pent 2,7
58:18 (59:17)	Pent 2,7
59:14 (60:12)	VI p P 2,5
61:2 (62:1)	JB, 10
61:11 (62:10)	AltBasCor, 1
63:6 (64:5)	VI p P 2,5
63:7-8 (64:6)	Asc 4,8
65:5 (66:5)	Asc 2,5
67:7 (68:6)	Asc 5,1
67:9-10 (68:8-9)	Pent 2,1
67:10 (68:9)	PP 2,2; PP 3,3
67:13 (68:12)	VI p P 2,1
67:36 (68:35)	VI p P 2,1
67:17 (68:16)	Asc 4,6
67:34 (68:33)	Asc 2,1
68:10 (69:9)	IV p P, 1
68:5 (69:4)	Asc 4,6
71:6 (72:6)	PP 2,2
71:9 (72:19)	Pent 1,6
73:12 (74:12)	Asc 2,1; Pent 2,4
76:3-4 (77:2-3)	Asc 6,8
76:3 (77:2)	Asc 2,4; Asc 6,14
76:4-5	VPP,3
76:4 (77:3)	Asc 4,9; 6,14
76:11 (77:10)	Pent 1,2; PP 3,1
78:13 (79:13)	Asc 2,6
79:6 (80:5)	VPP, 3; VI p P1,4
79:14 (80:13)	VI p P 1,3
83:2-3 (84:1-2)	Asc 4,9
83:6 (84:5)	Asc 4,4
83:7 (84:6)	VPP, 3
83:8 (84:7)	Asc 4,6; Asc 4,14

127:2 (128:2)	VI p P 1,4
129:7 (130:7)	PP 3,2
131:17 (132:17)	JB, 4
132:1 (133:1)	Asc 6,5
136:9 (137:9)	PP 3,3
138:6 (139:6)	Pent 1,1
138:17 (139:17)	PP 2,4; PP 2,5
140:4 (141:4)	Asc 1,3
140:5 (141:5)	PP 2,3
140:10 (141:10)	PP 3,6
141:4 (142:3)	Asc 4,9
141:8 (142:7)	VPP, 2
142:4 (143:4)	Asc 4,5
142:8 (143:8)	Pent 2,5
144:16 (145:16)	Asc 3,6; VI p P 1,2
145:8 (146:8)	Pent 2,8
147:12	Asc 6,4
147:14	Asc 6,4
149:7-8	Pent 3,1

Proverbs (Pr)

1:2	Asc 6,15
2:11	VI p P 1,4
2:14	VPP, 1; VI p P 1,1
6:3	Rog 1,1
10:28	Pent 2,1
11:26	VI p P 2,1
14:13	VPP, 3
16:4	Pent 3,4
25:16	VI p P 2,6
31:19	Asc 6,7

Ecclesiastes (Qo)

1:2	JB,7
1:3	JB,7
1:4	Asc 6,2; IV p P, 3
4:8	VI p P 1,3
4:12	PP 2,8; VI p P 2,6
7:30	AltBasCor, 1
9:1	Asc 2,5

24:20/27	Asc 3,9
24:29	VI p P 2,6
35:17	Asc 5,1
35:21	Asc 5,1
36:1	Asc 3,6; VI p P 1,2
36:15/18	Pent 2,4
40:20	Pent 3,1
44:10	PP 3,1; PP 3,4; PP 3,5
44:11	PP 3,6
44:12	PP 3,6
44:16	Asc 6,9
45:8/9	Asc 3,1
48:9	Asc 6,9
50:3	Pent 2,8
51:9	Asc 6,7

Isaiah (Is)

1:6	Pent 2,3
1:13	JB, 1
2:2	Asc 4,6
2:3	Asc 4,6
3:7	Rog 1,1
4:2	Asc 6,1; Pent 2,1
4:4	Asc 2,6; Pent 2,1
5:4	Pent 2,8
5:22	VPP, 1
6:3	Pent 1,6
9:2	Asc 6,10
9:6	Asc 4,1
11:1	Asc 6,1
11:2-4	Pent 3,1
11:2	PP 2,8
14:12-14	Asc 4,3
14:13	Asc 4,3
19:1	Asc 6,11
26:7	VPP, 2
38:10	VI p P 2,3
38:15	PP 2,7
38:16	Rog 1,2
40:6	IV p P, 3

Baruch (Ba)
   3:11   PP 1,4
   3:38   Asc 2,1; Asc 2,3; Asc 6,10; Asc 6,11;
                    Pent 2,7; Pent 2,8; VPP, 2
   4:36   Asc 4,7
   5:5   Asc 4,7

Ezekiel (Ezk)
   1:4   VI p P 2,5
   18:24   PP 3,6
   47:5   Asc 3,2

Daniel (Dn)
   7:9   Asc 6,1
   13:45   IV p P, 1

Hosea (Ho)
   2:7   JB, 11
   6:5   VPP, 4
   10:12   Pent 2,7

Amos (Am)
   5:1   PP 3,3
   6:6   IV p P,1

Micah (Mi)
   4:1   Asc 4,6
   4:2   Asc 4,6
   6:8   Pent 2,8
   7:5   IV p P 2,5
   7:6   IV p P 2,5

Habukkuk (Hab)
   2:3   Asc 5,1; 6,14

Malachi (Ml)
   3:1   JB, 6
   4:2   Asc 4,1

11:18	JB, 6; JB, 8
11:25	PP 1,5
11:29	Asc 6,11
11:30	Asc 3,6; PP 3,2
12:29	Pent 3,1
12:45	Asc 1,3
13:16	Asc 1,1; Asc 6,11
13:27-28	PP 2,3
14:4	JB,9
14:25	Asc 6,11
14:25-26	Asc 2,1
14:28-30	IV p P, 3
14:29	PP 1,2
14:30	Asc 2,3; PP 1,2; IV p P, 3; VI p P 2,5
16:17	PP 1,2
16:18	Pent 3,1
16:19	VPP, 4; PP 1,2
17:1	Asc 4,7
17:2	Asc 4,7
17:4	Asc 4,8; Asc 4,9; Asc 6,1; VI p P 2,5
17:6	Asc 4,9
17:27	Asc 2,1
18:12	Asc 6,13; Pent 2,5
18:20	JB,2
19:27	Asc 2,3; Asc 3,4; Asc 6,11; Asc 6,12; VPP,1
19:27-29	PP 1,5
21:7	PP 3,6
22:44	Asc 6,1
22:45	Asc 6,1
23:10	JB,1
24:28	Asc 4,1; JB,2
26:8-9	VI p P 2,4
26:10	Asc 1,3
26:24	PP 2,1
26:56	Pent 1,2
26:69-73	Pent 1,2
26:69-74	VI p P 2,4
26:75	PP 3,3
27:34	Asc 1,3

3:7	JB,9
3:8	JB,9
3:9	PP 2,1; PP 2,3
4:15	JB,3
4:18	Asc 6,10
5:5	IV p P,3
6:17	Asc 2,1
6:38	Asc 5,2; Asc 6,4; Pent 1,6
7:36-50	VI p P 2,4
7:39	VI p P 2,4
9:56	Asc 2,4
9:62	PP 3,2
10:18	Asc 4,3
10:20	Asc 2,5
10:23	Asc 6,11
10:27	JB,10
10:30	Asc 4,4; Asc 4,8
10:37	Asc 2,6; PP 3,4
10:40	VI p P 2,4
11:5-6	Rog 1,1
11:10	Rog 1,1
11:13	Asc 3,9; Pent 2,1
11:17	Asc 6,5
11:24	Pent 2,5
12:6	PP 3,6
12:32	Asc 5,1
12:35-36	Asc 6,4
12:49	Asc 6,15; JB,3
13:6-9	PP 2,1
13:8	PP 2,3
13:27	Asc 1,2
14:11	Asc 2,6
14:29	VI p P 1,2
16:8	VPP,1
16:19	Pent 3,5; JB,6
17:10	Pent 2,6
18:13	Asc 6,15
18:14	Asc 2,6
21:19	Asc 2,6
21:27	Asc 2,4

7:39	Pent 1,3
8:21	Asc 6,12
8:44	JB,9
9:24	Pent 1,5
11:11	PP 2,5
11:43	Asc 2,1
12:35	Asc 6,10
13:33	Asc 6,12
13:10	Pent 3,5
13:12	VI p P 2,1
13:36	Asc 2,3
14:2	Asc 2,3; Asc 4,9
14:2-3	Asc 4,1
14:6	Asc 2,6; VPP, 2
14:8	JB,2
14:12	Asc 3,5
14:16	Asc 6,2
14:17	Asc 6,12
14:18	Asc 2,3; Asc 3,6
14:23	Asc 3,9
14:26	Pent 1,5; Pent 2,6; Pent 2,7
15:1	Pent 3,1
15:13	Rog 1,1
15:15	Asc 6,11
15:26	Asc 3,9; Pent 2,1; Pent 2,6; Pent 2,7
16:5	Asc 6,15
16:6	Asc 3,4; Asc 3,8; Asc 6,12
16:7	Asc 2,3; Asc 3,4; Asc 4,1; Asc 6,12; Asc 6,13; Pent 3,2
16:8	Pent 1,3
16:13	Asc 3,9
16:20	Asc 3,4; Asc 3,8
17:3	Pent 1,1
17:5	Asc 6,1
18:22	Asc 2,1
18:37	PP 2,4
19:23	Asc 2,2; Asc 2,3
20:14-17	VI p P 2,4
20:17	PP 3,6
20:19	Asc 6,15; Pent 1,2

9:40	PP 1,2; PP 2,4
10:38	Asc 2,1
12:3-11	PP 2,4
12:10	PP 1,2
12:23	Pent 1,5
13:26	PP 2,1
17:30	Asc 6,10
18:3	PP 1,3
24:4	VI p P 1,4
24:25	Asc 6,2

Romans (Rm)

1:11	Asc 6,8
1:20	Asc 3,3; Pent 1,1
1:32	JB,9
2:4	Pent 1,1
2:6	Asc 1,2
3:23	PP 3,1
4:5	Pent 2,8
5:2	Asc 4,8
5:2-3	Pent 3,8
5:5	Asc 4,1; Pent 1,5
5:8	Asc 4,6
5:14	Pent 2,1
5:20	PP 3,2; VI p P 2,4
6:4	Asc 6,3; Asc 6,4; Pent 3,6
6:6	Asc 6,3
6:19	Asc 4,6
6:22	PP 2,3
7:1	PP 3,6
7:6	Pent 3,6
7:13	PP 1,1
7:15	IV p P, 2
8:1	Asc 1,3
8:3	Pent 2,1
8:5	Asc 6,13
8:13	AltBasCor, 4
8:15	Pent 1,4
8:16	Pent 2,6; Pent 3,8
8:17	Asc 6,4

7:31	Pent 3,4; IV p P, 4
8:1	Asc 4,4; Asc 4,5
9:26	PP 2,1
10:13	Asc 6,14; JB,8
10:17	VI p P 1,4
10:31	Asc 1,1
11:20-22	JB,1
12:3	VI p P 1,3
12:4	Pent 1,3
12:7	Pent 1,2
12:11	Pent 1,2
12:23-24	Asc 2,4
13:9	Pent 1,1
13:12	Asc 3,3; Asc 4,1
14:15	IV p P, 3
14:19	IV p P, 3
14:33	Asc 5,1
15:9	PP 3,1
15:10	Pent 1,5; VI p P 2,4
15:19	VI p P 1,2
15:44	Asc 6,2; Pent 1,6
15:50	PP 2,6

2 Corinthians (2 Co)

1:7	Asc 6,7
2:10	VPP, 4
2:15	Asc 2,5
3:6	IV p P, 3
3:15-16	Asc 6,10
3:18	Asc 4,9
4:15	Pent 3,4
4:18	JB,1
5:15	Asc 6,9; PP 3,5
5:16	Asc 6,12
6:5	Pent 2,6
6:10	JB,7
6:14	Asc 6,13
6:16	Asc 6,13
7:4	Asc 6,7
9:2	VI p P 1,1

| 6:12 | VI p P 2,5 |
| 6:16 | VI p P 2,5 |

Philippians (Ph)

1:11	Pent 3,8
1:23	Asc 3,6
1:24	Asc 6,12
2:7	Asc 4,6; Asc 6,15
2:9	Asc 2,6
2:10-11	Asc 2,2
3:13	AltBasCor, 2
3:20	Asc 4,1
3:21	Asc 2,4
4:7	Asc 6,4
4:8-9	Asc 6,6
4:13	Asc 5,2; PP 2,4
4:22-24	Pent 3,6

Colossians (Col)

1:9	Asc 6,14
1:18	JB,1
1:20	PP 1,1
2:3	Asc 2,2
2:9	Asc 2,2
2:13	Pent 1,4
2:14-15	Asc 2,1
2:18	IV p P 2
3:1	Asc 2,2
3:1-2	Asc 6,3-5; Asc 6,8
3:2	Asc 6,14
3:5	Asc 6,3
3:9-10	Pent 3,6
3:12	Asc 2,3; VPP,2
3:14	Asc 5,2

1 Thessalonians (1Th)

2:13	PP 2,3
4:4-5	Pent 3,7
4:17	Asc 6,2
5:4-5	VPP,1

6:5	Asc 6,10
6:7-8	PP 2,1
9:2-3	Asc 3,8
9:11	Asc 6,1
9:19	JB,11
9:28	Asc 6,1
10:7	Rog 1,2
10:31	JB,8; PP 1,1
11:6	Asc 1,2; Asc 3,5
11:26	PP 2,2
11:40	VPP,2
12:7	Asc 2,6
12:9	Pent 2,4; Pent 3,7
12:14	Pent 3,5
12:15	PP 2,3
12:22	Asc 5,2
13:13	VI p P 1,1

James (Jm)

1:6	Pent 1,4
1:14	Asc 3,7
1:17	PP 2,7
1:21	PP 2,8
1:23-24	VI p P 1,1
4:14	JB,7
4:17	Pent 1,5
5:17	VPP,3

1 Peter (1 P)

1:18-19	Pent 2,8
1:24	JB,7; IV p P,3
1:25	JB,7
2:20	Asc 1,3
2:21	VPP,3
2:22	PP 1,1
2:24	Asc 6,3
3:13	AltBasCor,3
5:5	AltBasCor,4
5:6	PP 3,1
5:7	Asc 5,1

CISTERCIAN PUBLICATIONS INC.
Kalamazoo, Michigan

TITLES LISTING

CISTERCIAN TEXTS

THE WORKS OF BERNARD OF CLAIRVAUX

Apologia to Abbot William
Five Books on Consideration: Advice to a
 Pope
Grace and Free Choice
Homilies in Praise of the Blessed Virgin
 Mary
The Life and Death of Saint Malachy the
 Irishman
Parables
Sermons on the Song of Songs I-IV
Steps of Humility and Pride

THE WORKS OF WILLIAM OF SAINT THIERRY

The Enigma of Faith
Exposition on the Epistle to the Romans
The Golden Epistle
The Mirror of Faith
The Nature and Dignity of Love

THE WORKS OF AELRED OF RIEVAULX

Dialogue on the Soul
The Mirror of Charity
Spiritual Friendship
Treatises I: On Jesus at the Age of Twelve,
 Rule for a Recluse, The Pastoral Prayer

THE WORKS OF JOHN OF FORD

Sermons on the Final Verses of the Song of
Songs I-VII

THE WORKS OF GILBERT OF HOYLAND

Sermons on the Songs of Songs I, II, III
Treatises, Sermons and Epistles

OTHER EARLY CISTERCIAN WRITERS

The Letters of Adam of Perseigne I
Baldwin of Ford: Spiritual Tractates
Guerric of Igny: Liturgical Sermons I-II
Idung of Prüfening: Cistercians and Cluniacs:
 The Case for Citeaux
Isaac of Stella: Sermons on the Christian Year
Serlo of Wilton & Serlo of Savigny
Stephen of Lexington: Letters from Ireland
Stephen of Sawley: Treatises

MONASTIC TEXTS

EASTERN CHRISTIAN TRADITION

Besa: The Life of Shenoute
Cyril of Scythopolis: Lives of the Monks of
 Palestine
Dorotheos of Gaza: Discourses
Evagrius Ponticus: Praktikos and Chapters
 on Prayer
The Harlots of the Desert
Iosif Volotsky: Monastic Rule
The Lives of the Desert Fathers
Menas of Nikiou: Isaac of Alexandra & St
 Macrobius
Pachomian Koinonia I-III
The Sayings of the Desert Fathers
Spiritual Direction in the Early Christian East
 (I. Hausherr)
The Syriac Fathers on Prayer and the Spiritual
 Life

WESTERN CHRISTIAN TRADITION

Anselm of Canterbury: Letters I-[II]
Bede: Commentary on the even Catholic
 Epistles
Bede: Commentary on Acts
Bede: Gospel Homilies
Gregory the Great: Forty Gospel Homilies
Guigo II the Carthusian: Ladder of Monks
 and Twelve Meditations
Peter of Celle: Selected Works
The Letters of Armand-Jean de Rancé I-II
The Rule of the Master

CHRISTIAN SPIRITUALITY

Abba: Guides to Wholeness and Holiness
 East and West
Athirst for God: Spiritual Desire in Bernard
 of Clairvaux's Sermons on the Song of Songs
 (M. Casey)
Cistercian Way (A. Louf)
Fathers Talking (A. Squire)
Friendship and Community (B. McGuire)
From Cloister to Classroom
Herald of Unity: The Life of Maria Gabrielle
 Sagheddu (M. Driscoll)
Life of St Mary Magdalene... (D. Mycoff)
Rancé and the Trappist Legacy (A.J.
 Krailsheimer)
Roots of the Modern Christian Tradition
Russian Mystics (S. Bolshakoff)
Spirituality of Western Christendom
Spirituality of the Christian East
 (T. Spidlék)

MONASTIC STUDIES

Community and Abbot in the Rule of St
Benedict I-II (Adalbert De Vogüé)
Consider Your Call: A Theology of the
Monastic Life (Daniel Rees et al.)
The Finances of the Cistercian Order in the
Fourteenth Century (Peter King)

Fountains Abbey and Its Benefactors
(Joan Wardrop)
The Hermit Monks of Grandmont
(Carole A. Hutchison)
In the Unity of the Holy Spirit
(Sighard Kleiner)
Monastic Practices (Charles Cummings)
The Occupation of Celtic Sites in Ireland by
the Canons Regular of St Augustine and the
Cistercians (Geraldine Carville)
The Rule of St Benedict: A Doctrinal and
Spiritual Commentary (Adalbert de Vogüé)
The Rule of St Benedict (Br. Pinocchio)
St Hugh of Lincoln (D. H. Farmer)
Serving God First (Sighard Kleiner)

CISTERCIAN STUDIES

A Second Look at Saint Bernard (Jean Leclercq)
Bernard of Clairvaux and the Cistercian
Spirit (Jean Leclercq)
Bernard of Clairvaux: Studies Presented to
Dom Jean Leclercq
Christ the Way: The Christology of Guerric
of Igny (John Morson)
Cistercian Sign Language
The Cistercian Spirit
The Cistercians in Denmark (Brian McGuire)
Eleventh-century Background of Citeaux
(Bede K. Lackner)
The Golden Chain: Theological Anthropology of
Isaac of Stella (Bernard McGinn)
Image and Likeness: The Augustinian
Spirituality of William of St Thierry   (David
N. Bell)
The Mystical Theology of St Bernard
(Étienne Gilson)
Nicholas Cotheret's Annals of Citeaux
(Louis J. Lekai)
William, Abbot of St Thierry
Women and St Bernard of Clairvaux
(Jean Leclercq)

MEDIEVAL RELIGIOUS WOMEN

Distant Echoes (Shank-Nichols)
Gertrud the Great of Helfta: Spiritual Exercises
(Gertrud J. Lewis-Jack Lewis)
Peace Weavers (Nichols-Shank)

STUDIES IN CISTERCIAN ART AND ARCHITECTURE
Meredith Parsons Lillich, editor

Studies I, II, III now available
Studies IV scheduled for 1991

THOMAS MERTON

The Climate of Monastic Prayer (T. Merton)
The Legacy of Thomas Merton (Patrick Hart)
The Message of Thomas Merton (Patrick Hart)
Solitude in the Writings of Thomas Merton
(Richard Cashen)
Thomas Merton Monk (Patrick Hart)
Thomas Merton Monk and Artist
(Victor Kramer)
Thomas Merton on St Bernard
Toward an Integrated Humanity
(M.Basil Pennington et al.)

CISTERCIAN LITURGICAL DOCUMENTS SERIES
Chrysogonus Waddell, ocso, editor

Cistercian Hymnal: Text & Commentary
(2 volumes)
Hymn Collection of the Abbey of the Paraclete
Molesme Summer-Season Breviary
(4 volumes)
Institutiones nostrae: The Paraclete Statutes
Old French Ordinary and Breviary of the
Abbey of the Paraclete: Text and
Commentary (5 volumes)

STUDIA PATRISTICA

*Papers of the 1983 Oxford Patristics Conference
Edited by Elizabeth A. Livingstone*

XVIII/1 Historica-Gnostica-Biblica
XVIII/2 Critica-Classica-Ascetica-Liturgica
XVIII/3 Second Century-Clement & Origen-
Cappodician Fathers
XVIII/4 *available from Peeters, Leuven*

TEXTS AND STUDIES
IN THE
MONASTIC TRADITION

*North American customers may order these books
through booksellers or directly from the warehouse:*

Cistercian Publications
St Joseph's Abbey
Spencer, Massachusetts 01562
(508) 885-7011

*Editorial queries and advance book information
should be directed to the Editorial Offices:*

Cistercian Publications
Institute of Cistercian Studies
Western Michigan University
Kalamazoo, Michigan 49008
(616) 387-5090

*A complete catalogue of texts in translation and
studies on early, medieval, and modern monasticism
is available at no cost from Cistercian Publications.*